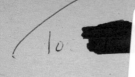

D0663164

A HOPE AND A FUTURE

With best wishes

Catherine

Mike Hare, Programme Director, Leaders-In-Training Programme,
Ontario Pioneer Camps, Summer 1987

A Hope and a Future

A young widow's
journey through grief

Catherine Hare

Hodder & Stoughton

LONDON   SYDNEY   AUCKLAND

First published in Great Britain in 1996

10 9 8 7 6 5 4 3 2 1

British Library Cataloguing in Publication Data
A CIP catalogue record for this title
is available from the British Library

ISBN 0 340 61250 9

Typeset by Palimpsest Book Production Limited,
Polmont, Stirlingshire
Printed and bound in Great Britain by
Cox & Wyman Ltd, Reading, Berkshire

Hodder and Stoughton
A division of Hodder Headline PLC
338 Euston Road
London NW1 3BH

Dedication

To Mike, a truly wonderful husband and father, and James, a son of whom his father would be proud, and my pride and joy.

'For I know the plans I have for you,' declares the LORD, 'plans to prosper you and not to harm you, plans to give you hope and a future.' (Jeremiah 29:11)

Contents

Acknowledgments   viii
Foreword by John Stott   ix
Introduction   xi
1 The Unexpected Happens   1
2 Tossed Back and Forth   19
3 A Surprise Blessing   35
4 Valley of Grief   55
5 Rituals and Reflections   75
6 Early Days   95
7 No Longer the Same   115
8 Letting Go   137
9 New Beginnings   155
10 A New Love?   169
11 A New Adventure   181
   Notes   195

Acknowledgments

I would like to thank Max Sinclair, who originally believed that I had a story worth telling, and Carolyn Armitage, who believed I could do it.

I could not have done it on my own; I was given much help. My editor at Hodder helped me think about what I should write; and Tony and Jane Collins, of Monarch Publications (and my bosses), have supported and encouraged me throughout the past year as I have re-lived each chapter. In particular, I would like to thank Jane for her helpful comments and suggestions on book structure. In addition, I would especially like to thank David Porter, who taught me some important aspects of writing and made valuable comments and suggestions on the typescript.

Lastly, I would like to thank my family and the many friends who shared my loss, and who have stood beside me in my grief, and without whose support I would never have come to the place where I felt able to write about Mike's death.

In a book such as this, it is impossible to include everyone who provided help and encouragement, or to record every incident. To those I have missed, please accept my sincere apologies – lack of inclusion here in no way means that your input or involvement was not helpful or important!

Foreword

Catherine Hare tells her story with great honesty, dignity and poignancy. There is much drama here, but no melodrama. As I read the manuscript, parts of the narrative brought tears to my eyes. What I admire most about Catherine's book is that she is always real. She neither exaggerates nor conceals. She is never glib.

Catherine allows us to enter with her into the whole gamut of emotions associated with bereavement – incredulity, grief, anger, self-pity, unbelief, confusion, loneliness and the sense of abiding loss. She helps us come to terms, as she has done, with the mysteries of God's providence, including his painful silences.

Rev Dr John Stott

Introduction

The death of a spouse, at any age, is an extremely traumatic event. In fact, the writers Holmes and Rahe, in their 'Life Stress Scale', identify the death of a spouse as the single most stressful life event that anyone can face. The death of any loved one is always difficult – the loss of a child is another extremely heart-wrenching and painful loss, and a bereavement through violent means is particularly shocking and distressing. Yet the loss of a life partner is different in its hardship, as it severs the spiritual, public, lifelong, emotional, social and economic commitment that two people have made to one another.

It should be said here that I also regard divorce as a type of bereavement. In some cases, a divorce is even harder to bear than a death, because it is a 'living death'. There is no clear-cut and final event to which to adjust; it is often messy; and the sadness of loss may be compounded by feelings of guilt and rejection as well. In addition, the pain can be prolonged by the ongoing contact necessary when there are children involved. An even further hardship, adding insult to injury, is the social stigma and lack of public acknowledgment of a bereavement such as divorce. But to examine all that would take a whole book on its own.

The uniqueness of the loss of a marriage partner is that it also includes other associated losses affecting all areas of life. In addition to the sorrow associated with the loss of a person's 'other half', a widowed person usually faces a myriad of other social and emotional losses. Widows and widowers may suffer a loss of social status: they are single again in a couple-oriented society; they often encounter financial insecurity – his/her partner no longer brings in an income; they frequently experience a loss of identity; and finally, they usually lose a sense of focus and purpose – they no longer have someone special to care for.

The grief of the widow or widower is particularly intense because of the intimacy of the marital relationship; in a good marriage, a spouse is one's closest companion, best friend, lover. The process of mourning is like a long and arduous journey through rough terrain, requiring much effort and persistence, for which few of us are prepared. In our 'instant society', we want immediate relief from our pain, but that belies the nature of such a bereavement. It is a long-term hurt, taking years rather than months for recovery to take place; and even then, the widow or widower will probably never be quite the same again.

Despite this, the process of readjustment after the death of a spouse is not insurmountable, as I hope to show in this book. This is my story, as a weak, ordinary person who has struggled through this process. I have been able to move forward with the help of a loving and compassionate God who has brought me much strength and healing. It is my prayer that any of you who also suffer losses of a similar kind, or face the loneliness of the single state or the challenge of single parenthood, will find encouragement in this story to walk forward step by step with trust in God, the source of all comfort.

1

The Unexpected Happens

'Since no man knows the future, who can tell him
what is to come? No man has power over the wind
to contain it; so no-one has power over the day of
his death' (Ecclesiastes 8:7–8).

The wind was howling through the trees around me,
nearly bending them to the ground with its immense force.
The waves were pounding the rocks with a mighty roar. I
shivered with cold, despite the dazzling sun reflected on
the water. The fierce wind had blown the snow into sharp
pointed drifts; the stones beneath my feet were slick with
ice. I hunted for a flat rock on which to balance, and then
raised my gaze to look out over the bay. The gale was
whipping my hair against my face; I needed to hold it
back so that I could see. As always, to my left was the
wide expanse of the bay. The promontory on the other
side of the sound was gleaming green and mauve in
the brilliant sun. My eyes followed the line of land to
my right where the sound narrowed as it funnelled into
the town.

I had stood on this shore, looking out over the lake,
every summer since the age of four. It never ceased to
give me a sense of security and stability. In sunshine or
rain, wind or calm, it remained constant and sure, solid
and permanent. This landscape had been there long before

I had come into the world, and would be there long after I had left it.

Usually, this lakeside picture evoked happy childhood memories of warm summer afternoons filled with hours of fun, swimming in the clear fresh water. But today, in cold mid-January, the scene was transformed. Beneath a bright-blue sky, the water lay murky grey-green. It hadn't yet completely frozen over, but there were hundreds of huge grey-white ice chunks floating everywhere. They were being tossed this way and that, crashing into one another. The waves were rushing faster and faster as if they were frantically trying to chase one another. No longer a familiar friend, the bay was now cold and forbidding. I felt frightened and helpless against nature's fury, and wanted to get back into the safe haven of our holiday cottage, where I knew it would be cosy and warm.

The evening before, my husband, Mike, and I had left the city in a terrific rush to collect Stacey, one of his university students, before driving north through the rolling country hills of southern Ontario to my grandparents' cottage for a weekend of skiing. Nine of his other students were also coming, but they were travelling up separately. Mike was the staff worker for McMaster University InterVarsity Christian Fellowship in Canada (IVCF), a Christian organisation that worked with students. In Britain this is known as the Universities and Colleges Christian Fellowship (of Evangelical Unions) (UCCF). Tall and athletic, Mike loved sport, and was always eager to enjoy the outdoors whenever the opportunity presented itself and to share his love of winter sports with others. So often we invited his students on these weekend retreats.

My grandparents' cottage is an ideal location for a retreat. Just a few hours' drive north of Toronto, it is nestled among the cedar, maple and silver birch trees of southern Ontario on Georgian Bay, the largest bay on the Great Lakes. It is also reasonably close to Blue Mountain, the tallest of the hills of the moraine left by glaciers formed during the Ice Age. Blue Mountain is a mere bump compared to the rugged heights of the Rockies in British Columbia, or to the French and Swiss Alps in Europe, but as we were only occasional skiers, we found it sufficiently challenging.

The previous weekend we'd also been away with some students. That time, though, it had not been to ski, but to go tobogganing and ice skating. Life seemed hectic – James, our first child, was barely two months old and we hadn't yet adjusted to the different lifestyle thrust upon parents by a newborn baby. I was still recovering from the physical strain of a long and difficult labour and delivery, and the exhaustion of continuous sleepless nights. With James in tow, even grocery shopping became a major event – I had to fit it in between his feeding times, collect all his paraphernalia (nappies and toys), and bundle him up in his snowsuit.

To go away for the weekend was no longer a simple matter of throwing things in a bag and jumping in the car. Since we'd become parents, packing had become a complicated affair whereby we needed to anticipate everything an infant might need. In addition, the journey itself was much more tiring, because James demanded my attention when he was crying or feeling restless.

Therefore I was feeling rather rushed and unprepared for our weekend away. We'd left the house in a complete tip, with the washing half done and the clean clothes still waiting to be put away. But I knew that Mike was eager to set off, so I bundled up our things and just left the mess behind.

After the three-hour or so journey (in a snowstorm) to the cottage, Mike finally stopped the car on the side of the road at the top of the cottage driveway, which wound down a steep slope, flattening out towards the lake. I stretched my legs with relief, as I stepped out of the car. 'Hmm,' I sighed. 'We've finally made it – I can't wait to get unpacked and settled in.'

Mike nodded. 'Yes, that was quite a drive. What a snowstorm! Oh well, at least it's stopped now – let's unpack.' He walked round to the back of the car to open the boot, and I leaned across the seat to unhook James from his baby seat. 'You're happy to get out of there, too, aren't you, little fellow?' I said. I tucked James's thick blanket in tightly around him to keep him warm while I carried him down to the cottage.

'Oh, no! I forgot my boots,' Mike exclaimed as he peered round at me from behind the car, wondering how he would be able to carry our cases through the deep snow. I looked down at my feet. 'Oh, oh! Me too!' We all laughed as Stacey looked sheepish and said, 'Er – me too!' Stacey was nearly as tall as Mike and very athletic. Somehow I didn't think snow would be much of a worry to her.

'Here, Catherine,' Mike called out, 'Why don't I go first and you follow in my footsteps – that might make it easier.' He bravely stomped down the hill, his big feet pointing outwards in his familiar lope as he made deep holes in the snow. I could barely follow in his steps – he was six foot and I'm five foot three – but somehow or other we gradually scrabbled our way down to the cottage. Suddenly, Mike stumbled as the snow reached up past his knees, and his bags went flying in all directions as he collapsed in fits of laughter. I smiled at his antics, and very carefully picked out my steps as I held James closely against me.

I stepped on to the porch, and reached for the door handle. It was locked. 'Oh no – I've forgotten the key,' I groaned. Mike smiled at me and shook his head. 'Oh, you wally!' He raised his gaze skyward; it wasn't the first time he'd noticed that I could be scatterbrained.

Fortunately, I quickly remembered that some friends of ours nearby had a spare key. 'We'll have to drive back to town,' I said apologetically. 'We'll never break into the cottage – it's always locked up very carefully for the winter.' Mike set down the bags and lifted James from my arms; we trudged back up through the snow to the car. Stacey decided to stay behind at the cottage to greet the others when they arrived.

By the time we got back to the cottage with the spare key, the other students had arrived and were trailing up and down the now well-trodden snow with sleeping bags and cases, waiting to be let in. They greeted us with shouts and laughter as we opened the door. The musty damp smell of the empty cottage was overpowering as I stepped inside. I set James down on the settee as I went round opening windows and switching on the lights and ceiling fans. 'Well, welcome to "the cottage". It's not very big and rather rustic – I hope we'll all fit in,' I said, as everyone dumped their belongings on the floor.

'No, it's great!' said one of the girls, then looked at me and asked, 'How are you, anyway? And how's James?' Just on cue, James started to wail.

'I'm fine thanks. James is hungry – I think I'd better feed him.' I took off my jacket and sat down.

Suddenly we heard a loud '*Oh no!*' and looked up. Mike peered out from behind the loo door. 'Catherine, the water isn't working!'

'Oh no!' I cried. 'The water pump must have frozen.' Mike gave me a knowing look, vividly recalling the occasion the previous winter when we had ventured to come to the cottage in freezing weather, and he spent days, numb with cold, replacing the water pump with my brother's help.

'We'll just have to make do,' Mike said. 'We can bring some water up from the lake for cooking and washing, and go to the loo behind a tree.'

A couple of the lads grabbed a bucket and found their way down to the lake to fetch water. Others started unpacking and getting the food out to make supper. I felt bad that things weren't as hospitable as they could be, and embarrassed that I couldn't remember all the students' names. I had met Mike's small group just a month earlier, when they'd visited us before Christmas, so I was reluctant to admit that I couldn't really remember their names. However, they all seemed happy and excited, and didn't appear to mind about the inconveniences.

After feeding James, I put him to bed and joined the others for supper. When we had finished the washing-up, we all congregated in the sitting-room, laughing and chatting. Everyone decided to go to bed early as the skiers wanted to make an early start in the morning, so we rolled out our sleeping bags on the floor. The five girls and I took ours into the bedroom with James, and the five boys and Mike remained in the sitting room. I wished I could have taken Mike aside to ask him some of the students' names, but instead joined the girls and quickly fell asleep, knowing I would soon be woken up by a hungry baby.

The following morning we were all rudely awakened by a jarring ringing at seven o'clock – Mike had set his watch alarm so there would be no late sleepers! I was still bleary-eyed after James's two o'clock feed, but dragged myself out of my sleeping bag and got dressed. Mike, in contrast, was in fine form, bright and eager for the day ahead. He wandered around cracking jokes and helping to make the breakfast.

After we'd cleared breakfast away, the students gathered together their skiing equipment and put on their long-johns. One of the students, Renate, tried on my ski boots: they fitted her perfectly. She was a quiet girl and I did not know her, but we smiled at each other shyly. Stacey stayed behind in the bedroom for a few extra minutes to read her Bible. I thought I ought to read a little as well, so opened my Bible and Notes. It was 16 January: James was exactly two months old today. Before I could read further, a cry interrupted me – James had woken up, wet and hungry.

By the time I had finished changing and feeding James, the others had left. Mike had been in and out a couple of times to pick up the skiing equipment and to load the vehicles, and all the students had left the cottage in ones and twos. 'Make sure no one breaks a leg!' I shouted. As I said it, I had a funny feeling that someone might, but brushed it off as me being silly. I thought Mike would come back to kiss me goodbye, but, in his eagerness to get on to the slopes and his desire to miss the crowds, he forgot.

I stayed back at the cottage to look after James and prepare supper for the skiers when they returned that evening. Only Dale remained behind with me. His parents and I both belonged to the Area Support Group of the McMaster University IVCF, and I knew they were active in a large church in Hamilton.

With James perched on one hip, I turned to Dale and said, 'Oh, have they all gone?' 'Yes, all set off,' he replied. I brushed aside my irritation at Mike not saying goodbye. I turned to Dale. 'Why didn't you go along too?' I asked.

'I came to bring my dad's minibus for them to use, and to stay behind with you!' he answered with a smile and a flourish. This was all very well, I thought to myself, but Mike should have better informed me of what was going on.

'I'll put James down for his nap and then I'll start the washing-up,' I said. 'I'll have to fetch some water from the lake first.'

'OK, I'll go to town and get another key cut so we can return this one,' Dale replied. I gave him the directions and off he went.

Once James was snuggled back into his cot, I bundled

into my winter jacket and carried a bucket down to the lake. On my trek down, I remembered Mike larking about before they left, and smiled to myself. Mike loved his job with IVCF, and enjoyed the students immensely.

We were so happy together, and we had just bought our first home in Hamilton a fortnight before James was born. His arrival was a deep joy for us both; I wished I could capture the moment and hold it for ever. I longed to spend more time with Mike and James as a family on our own; I wanted to savour each precious minute together. Life seemed rich and full, yet there seemed to be so little time to enjoy each other's company. There were always so many other people demanding Mike's attention.

As I balanced precariously on the rocks by the water's edge, I tried to fill the bucket with the icy water without pouring it over myself or falling in. It was tiring work, so I paused and looked up at the racing cotton-wool clouds and turbulence of the charging waves. Again and again I dipped the bucket between the rocks, and tried to catch as much water as possible with each oncoming wave. It took many feeble attempts, but I gradually filled the bucket enough to carry it back to the house. I made several trips, filling some saucepans for later use, as well as the washing-up bowl. By the time I'd finished, I was numb with the cold and my fingers were creased with red lines as a result of tightly clasping the wire handle of the bucket.

It wasn't long before Dale returned from town and helped me to do the washing-up while James slept. We chatted about the weather and other trivial things, and then Dale suddenly asked me a more personal question.

'What was it like, having a baby?'

'Do you mean the labour and delivery?' I queried. 'It was horrendous! I was in labour for thirty-six hours and hardly slept for three nights running. You know, I often hear women saying it was the most wonderful experience of their lives, but I found it awful. I was an emotional wreck for days afterwards – but at least we now have a wonderful son for all my efforts!'

'I guess, as guys, we've got it awfully easy,' Dale commented. 'We've no idea what you women have to go through.'

I ruefully agreed, then told him something that I'd never shared with anyone else. 'You know, it's weird, but I did a lot of thinking about death before I went into labour. I think I feel a little more prepared for it because of the birth. I looked at labour and delivery as a time to endure before the baby's birth, just like death is the passage through which we have to go before our new life with Christ.'

'Were you scared?' he asked.

I thought a moment before replying. 'Not in one sense – I mean, I had a pretty easy pregnancy, so I wasn't expecting to have any problems – but I was nervous about the unknown. It was scary having to face something that I'd never experienced before, and knowing that I had to go through with it. And there wasn't much I could do to prepare for it – I know Mike and I went to antenatal classes, but you still never know exactly what it will be like for you.'

Dale thought for a minute, then said, 'I guess most of us put off thinking about things like that till the time comes.'

He opened a can of scotch broth and found some bread rolls. I laid some plates, bowls and spoons on the table, and we sat down to eat our lunch. Just as we lifted our spoons of the steaming broth to our mouths, there was a knock at the door. Dale peered out of the window behind me, then glanced at me in surprise. 'It's two policemen!' he exclaimed.

I stood up, opened the door, and looked enquiringly at the two officers. They were wearing the dark-blue uniform of the Ontario Provincial Police and looked very official. One was tall and slim, while the other was short and stocky. Neither was smiling.

'Can we come in?' asked the tall one. They made me nervous, but I didn't feel I could refuse them entry.

As they walked into the kitchen, they took off their hats. Ignoring me, the taller one turned to Dale and asked, 'Do you own a blue minibus?' He quoted the registration number.

'Yes, it's my dad's,' replied Dale. 'He let me borrow it for the weekend so that some of my friends could use it to go skiing.' I felt a little miffed that they were not addressing me – after all, I was the 'lady of the house'. But then I assumed that it had nothing to do with me – it seemed to be Dale's minibus that was the problem.

The tall officer spoke again. 'The vehicle has been involved in an accident.' I still couldn't quite work out why they had come all the way to the cottage to tell us this.

The officer looked serious, and repeated, 'A very bad accident. Two have been killed, and the rest have been taken to hospital.'

At first, I just couldn't grasp his meaning. I didn't even know that all of the skiers had gone together in the minibus. All the vehicles were parked up on the road, hidden by trees. Then gradually it began to dawn on me what he was saying. 'Oh God! No! Mike!', I thought. In a trembling and terrified voice, I heard myself ask, 'Who were the ones who were killed?'

The shorter officer then spoke: 'We don't know for sure, but we think one of them was the driver: Mike, I think his name was.'

My world stopped. Suddenly I felt totally alone. It was as if I was back on that howling, turbulent shore. The crash of the waves and the roar of the wind echoed in my ears. The wind was pushing and pushing me. I was helpless, being pulled by the current . . .

No! Not Mike! It can't be! My mind completely rebelled at such a terrible thought. Yet at some deeper level of awareness I knew that what they were saying was true. It was almost as if I had always known that one day I would experience such a hardship. But now the moment had arrived, and I wasn't ready. I felt utterly helpless; there was nothing I could do to stop this terrible thing from being so.

I burst into tears. It all seemed totally unbelievable – Mike was so alive such a short while ago. He *couldn't* be dead, but yet he was. In between my racking sobs, I cried, 'He's my husband! We have a two-month-old son! What's to become of him?' The officers looked taken aback. I don't think they realised that they were coming to inform the wife of a fatality of the crash.

Eventually the sobs subsided enough for me to ask them how the accident happened. The tall officer explained, 'They were driving along the Meaford Road, when it looks as if they came to a clearing and swerved on to the oncoming lane and hit a lorry head-on. The driver of the minibus slammed on the brakes and tried to get back into his own lane, but didn't . . . The girl behind him was killed instantly; the driver had head injuries and died later in hospital.' The lorry driver wasn't badly injured, but he was pretty shaken up.

Quietly, Dale asked, 'Do you know who the girl was, the one who was killed?'

The shorter officer said, 'No – all the others were injured too. They were sent to different hospitals, and we haven't been able to get the information from them yet. It took us three hours to find you here. None of the survivors knew who owned the cottage.'

Gravely, the tall officer turned to Dale and asked, 'Please could you come with us to identify the bodies?'

'Can I see Mike?' I cried out. I wanted to go to him so badly.

The officers hesitated. 'I think we should identify the girl's body first. They're in two different hospitals – there wasn't enough room for all of them in the local hospital, so some were sent to the central district hospital. In fact, two of the girls have spinal cord injuries, and so were taken by helicopter to Sunnybrook Hospital in Toronto. Perhaps if Dale here comes with me to identify the girl at the central hospital first, then we can sort something out.'

I gasped. Spinal cord injuries? Were they going to die too? Be paralysed for life? Where was God? Why didn't God prevent it? I cried out inside, 'Oh God, Help!' I was bewildered with shock, but even then I wanted to face reality and not deny the facts. Dale then left with the short officer, and the tall one stayed behind with me.

At that moment, James started to cry and I automatically picked him up and sat down to feed him. The officer looked uncomfortable and said, 'My daughter is about the same age as your son.' I caressed James's forehead as I fed him and fresh tears came to my eyes. It suddenly hit me that James would never see his father again. My mind flashed back to my recent preoccupation with death.

I recalled a strange prayer that I'd prayed after Mike and I had been trying to conceive for a couple of months. When I discovered with disappointment that I wasn't pregnant, a sudden panic and sense of urgency gripped me. I had a strong feeling that if I didn't get pregnant soon, I would never have the chance. I had cried out to God, 'Before you take Mike, please could I have a son?' Just one month later, I was overjoyed to discover that I was pregnant. It was a shock to realise that my prayer had been answered. I now had a son, but without his father. It broke my heart to think that James would never know his father in the way that I did. He would never enjoy his sense of fun, or receive his guidance and love.

Strangely, I found myself trying to encourage the officer. 'We are Christians,' I said. 'I know that Mike is with God.' Again I broke down, and had to stop feeding James as I sobbed and sobbed. I turned to James and said, 'I promise to tell you all about your daddy.'

I then telephoned my parents in Toronto to tell them the terrible news. My father picked up the phone. I hardly knew how to begin. 'Dad, I have some dreadful news. Mike has been killed in a car accident.' He broke down at the news and handed the phone to my mother. I explained to them what little I knew.

Without hesitation, my mother said, 'Stay put, and we'll come. Don't go to the hospital yet – we'll take you there when we arrive.'

I then had the terrible task of telling Mike's parents in England. I rang and rang, but there was no answer. I knew there was a big time difference between Canada and England, but wasn't sure what time it was or what they would be doing. Finally, I got through to Mike's brother, David, who lived in Reading. I broke the news to him and he promised to try to reach his parents as soon as possible. I gave him the cottage's phone number so that they could get back to me.

It wasn't long before Dale returned with the news that it was Renate who had died. He'd got the details of where everyone else was, so that we could visit them. The officers then left, and Dale and I just stood there, wondering what to do next. I told Dale that I'd telephoned my parents, and that they were going to come to the cottage as soon as they could. Dale then rang his parents.

Just as he hung up, the phone rang. Mike's parents, Douglas and Ann, had by now heard the news from David. 'Catherine, we've heard the terrible news from David. What exactly happened?' It must have been so hard for them to know what to say to me. 'How are you coping? Do you have someone with you?'

I reassured Mike's parents. 'Yes, one of the students is with me, and my parents will be here soon. We'll go to the hospitals when they arrive – I'll ring you again later.'

Dale and I cleared up the uneaten lunch, then sat down and did the only thing we felt we could do. We prayed together, 'Oh Lord, we know that Mike and Renate are with you. Please bring healing to the injured students. Please be with us all and help us.'

It was a very long afternoon. We packed up the students' belongings and tried to identify what belonged to whom. My former minister and dear friend, Dr Samuel Baxter, rang me, having just heard the news. 'Catherine, I'm so terribly sorry. You are in our thoughts and in our prayers. If there is any way at all in which we can help, please don't hesitate to contact us.'

I put James back down for a nap, crying on and off for the rest of the afternoon. My parents finally arrived in the evening. They had driven up with Pat and Jack, my sister-in-law's parents, who lived close by. My father hugged me and we cried together. Mum and I clung to each other, quietly sharing the shock of the loss of Mike. They didn't have to say very much; their love and care was shown in their hugs and the fact that they had come.

Dale identified which hospitals the other students were in, and we packed up everyone's belongings. James had by now gone to sleep for the night, so I tried not to wake him as I bundled him up and carried him out to the car. In some ways it was a help that he was so young; he couldn't comprehend what was happening. At least I didn't have to deal with his grief as well as my own.

On our journey to my parents' home in Toronto, we stopped at the two hospitals and visited the injured students. I wanted to see Mike, to face fully the fact of his death. I needed to be sure that they hadn't made a mistake.

First we visited the two students at the Owen Sound local hospital. They didn't know that Mike had been killed, so we decided not to tell them at this point. They had each suffered broken legs. After visiting them, we were directed back down to the main floor where we were met by two police officers. They suggested that we sit down for a while in a side room before identifying Mike's body. The older officer started talking to my parents about what had happened.

'I expect they were speeding – you know what kids are like these days,' he said.

'Speeding?' I questioned. 'But the officers who came to the house said they were within the speed limit – 50 m.p.h.'

'Yes, but their speed was probably excessive for the road conditions,' he answered brusquely.

What road conditions?, I wondered. It was bright and sunny – not snowing or dark. It was only nine o'clock in the morning. They certainly hadn't been drinking or fooling around. They were simply on their way to go skiing.

The police officer must have noticed my expression of doubt and said, 'There was a terrific amount of snow blowing across the road. The township had to close off the road for six hours after the accident, in order to clear it.'

I was deeply offended that he was talking so glibly about my husband. Mike was certainly not an irresponsible young student. He was the students' staff worker, and I knew him to be a careful and responsible adult.

My mother was equally indignant, and she quickly challenged the police officer. 'Mike was very responsible – he wasn't in any way a careless person!'

Yet perversely, I wanted my mother to remain quiet.

I didn't want to try to minimise the situation or protect myself from its severity. But despite our statements defending Mike, I did feel real guilt on Mike's behalf. There were so many seriously hurt. I even pondered on a mercy in Mike's death – at least he didn't have to live with the guilt and feelings of responsibility of another person's death, and many injured, as a result of his driving – even if such guilt was unjustified.

Already, I missed Mike so much. I longed to hold him, to touch him and to talk to him. 'Could I see his body now?' I asked quietly.

The policeman replied gravely, 'I don't recommend it – he's pretty badly injured; he took the impact on his face.'

'His face?' I sobbed and sobbed again as the impact of the accident sunk in. In the end, my parents went to identify his body and I stayed with Pat. I turned to her, 'I just want to see him, to know they didn't make a mistake – to say goodbye. He never said goodbye to me this morning.'

After a short while, my parents returned; they were very quiet and subdued. I asked my father if Mike had seemed at peace.

He hesitated, then answered slowly, 'Yes, he was. But I only saw one side of his face. Catherine, we don't think you should see him.'

Rather insensitively, the younger policeman tried to help, and said, 'Probably the funeral people can fix him up, and then you could see his body then.' By now, my mind was conjuring up gruesome visions of ghastly mutilation, but I quickly repressed these thoughts and told myself that I was going to remember Mike as he was. I decided that perhaps it was best for me not to see Mike's body at this point.

Next we stopped at the Meaford Hospital. The students there had various injuries: cuts, bruises, fractured bones and internal injuries. They already knew about Mike's and Renate's deaths. I was touched by their love and care for me when they had their own shock and injuries to contend with. I was horrified by the seriousness of the students' injuries; but at least they were alive.

We finally arrived at my parents' home in Toronto at three o'clock in the morning. We walked into the kitchen to find the entire table laden with food prepared by a friend of my mother, Betty Lou.

I felt utterly exhausted and went straight upstairs to put James and myself to bed. I lay James down in his cot in one room and slipped under the covers in the bed in the spare room, totally drained. Yet I couldn't sleep. Mike was *dead* – I could barely grasp it, yet knew it was true. Death was so irrevocable, so final. There was no room for bargaining or pleading; my beloved husband was gone, and he was never coming back. How I longed to go to him to hug him and hold him, talk to him. But I couldn't; there was a great chasm between us that couldn't be crossed. 'If only I had been in the minibus too,' I thought.

Yet I didn't really want to face death; it seemed dark and mysterious. I suddenly realised that, until now, I had been sheltered from death. Most of my relatives lived in Britain. When my paternal grandmother had died, when I was twelve, I was deeply saddened. She had come over to visit us a couple of times, and I had fond memories of her cuddly, ample bosom and the numerous games of whist that we played together. Yet because she lived so far away, the impact of her death was muted. Only my father went to Britain for the funeral; and her dying made little difference to our daily routine.

This, though, was totally different. Death was so near; I could feel its cold breath raising the hairs on the back of my neck. I was in unfamiliar territory. It terrified me, and I just wanted to curl up in the security of the blankets to wake up and find that it was all just a dreadful nightmare that would be over by the morning. The shelter of being back at my parents' home gave me a certain sense of comfort, but I knew that my parents couldn't protect me from the reality of my loss; it was something I would need to face on my own.

In desperation, I called out to God in the darkness, 'Where are you, God? Why didn't you prevent this accident? Don't you care? Have you led me this far, just to abandon me now?' These questions buzzed around and around in my head, until eventually I must have fallen asleep through total exhaustion.

2

Tossed Back and Forth

'If any of you lacks wisdom, he should ask God . . .
But when he asks, he must believe and not doubt,
because he who doubts is like a wave of the sea,
blown and tossed by the wind' (James 1:5–6).

I was born in 1958 in western Canada, one of triplets. My
brother, Stuart, arrived first, then came my sister, Fiona. I
was the last of the litter – but not the smallest. My brother
was the heaviest at 4 lb 3 oz, I weighed a middling 3 lb
15 oz, and my sister was the smallest at 3 lb 8 oz. We
had been born six weeks prematurely and needed to be
kept in hospital incubators until we gained weight.

It was my mother's first pregnancy and she had no
idea that she was carrying triplets. However, by about the
seventh month of pregnancy she noticed that her abdomen
was becoming unusually large, and asked her obstetrician
if she could be having twins. He insisted that he could hear
only one heartbeat, so assumed that there was only one
foetus. No one was more astonished than her obstetrician
when she actually delivered three babies!

Neither of my parents had a history of multiple births
in their families, nor had my mother taken any fertility
drugs; we were apparently a 'gift of nature'. As fraternal
triplets, we looked no more alike than ordinary brothers
and sisters. Identical triplets are relatively uncommon,

but fraternal triplets even more so: a one in 35,000 occurrence.

My parents were of British descent: Dad was born on the Isle of Skye, and Mum was born in Newcastle upon Tyne and grew up in Glasgow. They emigrated from Scotland independently; my mother with her family, and my father on his own. They first met at a church young people's group in a small town in northern Ontario. For over five years they went out together, while my mother finished her nursing training. When my father, a sales engineer for a firm dealing in equipment for oil, gas and mining industries, was promoted to regional manager, they got married. Their honeymoon was the long drive across the vast flat wheat fields of the Prairies, to Edmonton, Alberta, in the foothills of the Rockies. My mother became pregnant almost immediately after their marriage, and the three of us arrived early, just eight months later.

At first my mother was thrilled and excited about having triplets, and missed us terribly while we were kept in hospital for several weeks for observation and treatment. She waited impatiently until the paediatricians declared us fit enough to come home, but then she faced the daunting task of caring for three small infants at once. It was a tremendous load, especially as my father often had to go away on business trips, and so Mum was left with the bulk of the work.

Nor did the work let up as we grew into healthy toddlers, because before my parents could catch their breaths, two years later they had a second son, and the following year a third – five children under four! It was utterly exhausting. As a large family of so many young children, our lives were characterised by non-stop activity. Our closeness in ages forced us to co-operate right from the start. Whenever one of us wanted a biscuit, he or she would automatically ask for five and pass them around to the others. For we children, who knew nothing else, it was great fun: we always had the company of each other as playmates and enjoyed the stimulation and fun of playing games, making crafts and going on walks together.

At this stage, my parents did not go to church regularly. Obviously it was difficult to go to church with so many babies and young children in tow — but, even so, we triplets were christened as infants at a local church.

When we turned four, Dad was transferred to Toronto, Ontario. We moved into a neighbourhood that was full of other young families. This was a great relief to my mother, who could now get out of the house and mix with other young mothers while we children extended our play to friends as well as siblings.

When we triplets started school, we were each put in different classes. The teachers meant well by trying to treat us as individuals rather than a group, but it gradually divided us as we developed other friendships and had different school experiences. Soon we stopped co-operating, and instead we started competing. In the first couple of years I found school work easier than Fiona and Stuart, and felt superior to them when I progressed faster in maths and reading.

We moved house again when I was seven, this time still within Toronto, and after we'd settled into a new school, Mum began taking us five children to a church nearby. My two younger brothers were christened there. I enjoyed the ceremony and ritual; Christianity seemed, to me, to be learning to be good and kind. God was like a heavenly grandfather, sometimes stern and at other times indulgent. I thought Jesus was a good man. My favourite part of church was the singing.

A few years later, a new church was built next to our home, at the end of a cul-de-sac. My sister Fiona and I joined the Sunday school, and a weekly girls' group called Pioneer Girls. I was fascinated by the personal way people spoke about God at this church. God seemed so real and alive to them; and their faith seemed to be really important to them, affecting the whole of their lives. I started to wonder if my parents really were Christians, as we never prayed or talked about God at home. Religion seemed to be a private matter best kept to oneself.

Friends soon became all-important to me. I had the ability to do well at school, but was easily distracted and failed to put much effort into my studies. My motivation to learn had to compete with my desire to be popular and accepted, and I let my school work suffer in order to socialise.

My girlfriends were not Christians, and had older sisters who seemed to know far more about the world than I did. They seemed so sophisticated and I yearned to be like them – yet I also longed to be like the leaders of the Pioneer Girls. It was the beginning of a struggle that would last throughout my maturing years.

On Sundays I worshipped God and promised to be good for the next six days – then during the week I squabbled with my friends and ignored God altogether. I lived in two separate worlds and felt comfortable in neither. At school I didn't feel respected or appreciated by my friends; at church I felt guilty and inferior.

I started to smoke at the age of eleven, when a friend offered Fiona and me cigarettes from a pack she'd stolen from her parents. We were each invited to try one. My sister backed off and said she didn't want to smoke. I, on the other hand, considering my sister a 'chicken', took a cigarette in my fingers and tried to copy my girlfriend's actions. I had never seen my parents smoke, so I was not sure what to do. I took the tiniest puff possible. My friend teased me, accused me of being naïve and ignorant, then showed me how to inhale. I tried to copy her by taking a deep breath, which promptly sent me into spasms of coughing and spluttering. However, after my first embarrassing attempt, with a little practice I became an acceptable smoker – and we often sneaked down to a tree house at the end of the road to have a cigarette. It gave me a wonderful sensation of being wicked and worldly. On one occasion, my father noticed the smell of tobacco clinging to my hair and coat, but I denied doing such a naughty thing as smoking and blamed it on the people we were with. Thus began my life of secrecy and deceit.

Repeated prayers and confessions were frustrating and seemingly futile. Yet I was learning at the church that God loved me just as I was, even if I was disobedient. Sunday school teachers told me that Jesus had died so that I could be forgiven for my sins, and accepted by God. I learned that no one was completely good, that no one could earn his or her way into heaven by good behaviour. The leaders taught me that it was faith in Christ that put us right with God, not good works. In spite of my rebelliousness, I did believe in Jesus and considered him my Saviour. Yet I failed to extend this intellectual assent to the whole of my life, and to recognise that it also required a commitment to follow Jesus and obey his commands. In my confusion I remained aloof, and continued to maintain a secular lifestyle with my school friends.

Like many adolescents, I longed to be affirmed by my peers. On the surface, I was outgoing and an extrovert. I was a petite blonde, lively and vivacious, and my parents and teachers were always complaining that I talked too much. I loved going places and joining in group activities, cycling and playing sports. Yet underneath all this activity, I hid deep insecurities. I was a late developer and felt very self-conscious at my lack of physique. At the age of twelve I still looked like a ten-year-old, and had not yet developed breasts or womanly hips. On top of all this, I became very conscious that my body was not symmetrical: one hip stuck out more than the other, and one side of my waist went in more than the other. It was not until I had a baby of my own that I learned that I suffered from a mild form of scoliosis, curvature of the spine. I always wore baggy clothes to cover up my self-consciousness about my appearance. This only added to my feelings of inferiority, as I didn't wear mini skirts or other fashionable clothes like my friends did.

By the age of fourteen, though, I had physically matured and felt more self-confident. At high school, I started going to parties and dances with girlfriends. A couple of my girlfriends already had boyfriends, and I hoped that I too would meet someone special. I did meet boys at school and at the parties, but usually the ones I liked weren't interested in me, and the boys who showed interest in me weren't my type.

However, during the course of my teenage years there were some exceptions to this rule, and eventually I progressed beyond the initial awkwardness and feelings of discomfort in male company to go out on dates. These friendships rarely lasted longer than a few months, but I started drinking alcohol at parties. I enjoyed male companionship and affection, but any pleasure or contentment was fleeting as it was tinged with guilt and the fear of disapproval.

At the same time, I turned to the church for acceptance and joined the youth group there. It warmed my heart to learn that God loved me, but I never felt as though I really belonged to this group either. Most of the young people there were several years older than me, and I failed to develop any close friendships. Nevertheless, I continued to attend the Pioneer Girls' group and enjoyed the crafts and activities and the wholesome Christian atmosphere. Yet secretly, I still felt different, 'worldly', and struggled with conflicting feelings of admiration for their goodness while at the same time feeling contempt for their strict rules.

The only time I felt peaceful and at ease with myself was each summer when, as a family, we would go to my maternal grandparents' cottage on Georgian Bay. At the lake, there was no competition for approval nor any pressure of studies. Without other friends to play off my sister and I against one another, we got along quite well. As a family, we spent most of our time swimming and playing tennis. On rainy days we spent hours playing games and puzzles. There were no parties to go to, no people to tempt me to smoke or drink, and no boys to distract me. We also had special tea parties with my grandmother, occasions when she would allow us to use her best bone china.

Yet each autumn, we had to return to the city and to the peer pressure and social competition. This tension only seemed to increase when, at the age of seventeen, I found myself a steady boyfriend, Mark. To start with, it all felt wonderful. It was very flattering to meet someone special who I was very attracted to, and who – incredibly – seemed to like me as much as I liked him. It was wonderful to feel that I finally belonged to a popular and 'cool' group. Yet the companionship and acceptance failed to remove my inner discontent, and eventually I realised that even such a close friendship was not enough to meet my innermost needs. However, it took some four years of building tension before I finally chose one life over the other.

Mark was tall, dark, athletic and handsome. A girl-friend and I first noticed him when he was kicking a football around with his friends. They invited us to a party that evening where Mark and I talked non-stop and realised our mutual attraction.

The first time we went out together, he took me to an ice-hockey game. He introduced me to his friends and their girlfriends and I quickly became part of their group. We went to parties every weekend, smoked cigarettes and drank alcohol. I thought I was cool, sophisticated, aware. Yet my parents gradually became worried about the bad influence of some of the wilder youngsters, and set strict rules. I rebelled by breaking their curfews, and so was repeatedly 'grounded'.

Mark and I had great fun together: we played tennis, did homework, went out for meals, attended concerts and spent much time with his older brother and sister. We both found part-time jobs at a local grocery store and often went out with friends after work. Yet guilt at times crept into the relationship when we began skipping school to go to his house. Deep down, I knew I was being a hypocrite.

I talked to Mark about my belief in God and tried to get him to come to church, but he always refused. During the next four years I increasingly struggled with my inconsistency in lifestyle and beliefs, and eventually started refusing to join in the drinking and smoking. Mark and I slowly began to drift apart, and started arguing over our clashing values. He couldn't understand why I no longer wanted to do certain things. Yet because we were so used to being together, we continued to go out with each other. My guilt and confusion only intensified when my mother started going to church and came to a real faith in Christ. Suddenly it seemed that God was really alive and working in people's lives.

In the meantime, my friendship with Mark muddled along. We rowed, then patched things up, and I managed to ignore the gap that was developing between the world of our relationship and that of my home and family.

The following summer I stayed in Toronto instead of going to Georgian Bay, in order to work full time to save up for university; and it was during that period that Mark proposed and I accepted. He bought me a stunningly beautiful eleven-diamond engagement ring. My mother was away at my grandparents' cottage at the time. I was very upset when my parents failed to be joyful at our news – the more so because I myself was still uncertain about the relationship. Over the next few months I began to feel more and more confused and unhappy. Instead of feeling the excitement that I had expected, I was in emotional turmoil. I didn't know who to turn to – Mark's friends didn't understand my problem, and I didn't think that anyone from my church would be objective enough to talk to. So instead, I worried and fretted on my own.

In September, I started studying social work at university. It was hard work, but seemed to suit me – I was interested in people, and their thinking and behaviour. I began to grasp the complex way that people are shaped by social customs, economic class, culture, family background and their individual hopes and dreams. The course fitted my interests and abilities, and I enjoyed developing skills in counselling.

By this time, I knew in my heart that God was unhappy about me marrying Mark – I well knew the verse in Scripture that said, 'Do not be yoked together with unbelievers' (2 Corinthians 6:14). When I was being honest with myself, I knew that when I was with Mark I was far from God, and that being with him pulled me down spiritually. Yet I was afraid to let go of the security of our relationship and to trust God with my future. We had by now been planning to get married for four years, and I didn't think anyone else would find me attractive. I was terrified of being alone, afraid that God would want me to be a spinster, a single missionary in a far-off land like Africa.

My internal struggle came to a head a few days later, during another working afternoon in a lull between customers. I was standing, gazing out of the store window, yet seeing nothing because I was lost in my unhappy thoughts. Finally, I admitted to myself how miserable I felt. 'God, I can't stand it any longer,' I prayed. 'I give up. I hate my life. I wish I were dead. Surely it can't be worse following you. I'll do what you want. I will break up with Mark and trust that you have something else in store for me. I will follow you even if it means being on my own.' It wasn't exactly the prayer of a willing and eager convert, but to my great surprise an indescribable peace and joy flooded through me. What a relief it was to be rid of such inner conflict and to feel an unconditional acceptance and forgiveness. I knew that it was the right decision, and felt a great assurance that life would somehow be all right.

The next time I saw Mark was at his parents' home when his parents were away. It was difficult, but I took a deep breath and broached the subject directly: 'Mark, you know how unhappy I am – we both are – with all our quarrels and fights. We've talked about this over and over again and have got nowhere. I can't be inconsistent with my Christian beliefs any longer. I can't marry you.'

Mark looked very distressed and pleaded with me. 'Catherine, give us a chance. I'll change. I'll do what you want – I'll become a Christian. I don't know why it's such a big deal for you anyway.'

'No, Mark. It won't work. I hope you will become a Christian, but it can't be for me – that's between you and God.'

Mark was hurt and angry and kept trying to persuade me to change my mind, but I remained firm. I returned his ring and walked home. I felt sad, but at the same time I felt relieved. My parents said little when they heard the news of our broken engagement, yet I knew that they felt it was the right decision.

My grandfather, who came to stay with us at weekends, was more overt in his approval of my decision, and approached me one morning, saying, 'I'm proud of you. It is not easy to break off an engagement, but you must never feel pressured into marriage if you're not sure you are right for each other.' I knew he was right. I had no second thoughts nor vacillations concerning my decision. Without a shadow of doubt, I knew that I had done the right thing, and my feelings of relief and peace confirmed my decision and gave me courage to look forward to a different future.

At university, there seemed to be a greater freedom to be oneself than at high school – I no longer felt swayed this way and that, pushed to conform, or follow the crowd. Certainly some students were wild and rowdy, others were fairly 'straight-laced', and many more were somewhere in between. Also, I felt stronger in myself and able to be different from others if need be. I made some new friends, but didn't get too involved in the university social life because I commuted from my parents' home to save money.

My developing Christian beliefs were often challenged by tutorial discussions on socialism, communism and Marxism, yet I started to gain confidence to question my lecturers' assumptions. I tried to consider social issues from a Christian perspective. Sociology classes were a challenge, and I often became confused. I felt that I needed to talk to some other Christians who were also struggling with different 'isms'.

One day I saw a notice on a wall about the Ryerson Varsity Christian Fellowship. I entered the meeting a little hesitantly, but was warmly welcomed by a lovely girl who turned out to be a fourth-year social work student. She introduced me to the student president, who was completely bald. He had a sparkling personality, and we started chatting and quickly discovered that we had mutual friends and acquaintances from my home church. It was only later that I learned that he had cancer and didn't have long to live.

The Ryerson VCF invited me to a Christian missionary conference to be held during the Christmas break, whose main speaker was Dr John Stott. Tall and slim, and dressed formally in suit and tie, Dr Stott seemed polite and detached. Yet his graciousness and unassuming manner seemed only to enhance the clarity and power of his words. To me, he seemed so incredibly 'English'. He taught with intellectual integrity and sound logic, and this appealed both to my mind and to my spirit. I felt as if I was being 'transformed by the renewing of [my] mind' (Romans 12:2). Some of his words still stand out in my memory: 'We are all called to be witnesses, to encourage others, by word and action, to become followers of Christ . . . We are to be salt and light in the world: salt, to hinder its decay; light, to spread the gospel of the truth of Christ and to frame our manner of life in a way that is worthy of the gospel . . . no matter where our location, or what our occupation, we have a responsibility to share the good news of God's love and forgiveness to others.' It was as though God was speaking directly to me. In one fell swoop, Dr Stott shattered my understanding of a missionary as a dowdy misfit in society. In contrast, he painted a picture of a missionary as someone who has the privilege and honour of showing God's love to others.

By the end of the conference, I realised that following God was not a poor second, but rather a high and holy calling. I knew that I didn't have to worry about the future, whether I was to remain single or get married, whether I was to stay at home or go abroad, for being a Christian gave ultimate meaning and purpose to my life. I could instead concentrate on serving God now, where I was, and trust that God would lead me step by step.

It took a little time to adjust to my new future without Mark, and it took him a while to understand why I felt I needed to break up with him. But unbeknown to me, some people had been praying for me, including my Pioneer Girls camp leader, Jessica, from the previous year. She and I both lived in Toronto, but at different ends of town and we went to different churches. About a year after Mark and I broke up, two years since I had been to camp, we unexpectedly met up at a Christian meeting. Jessica came up to me and asked me outright if I'd broken up with Mark yet. Amazed, I asked her how she knew about my struggle with this decision. She explained that she had been praying for me for over a year. I happily reported that her prayers had been answered months ago, and she was now free to pray for someone else!

During my studies I worked part time for a while as a social worker with mentally handicapped people, and then later with homeless people in inner-city Toronto. It was rewarding to play a part in encouraging people facing various crises, and to see some of them face tremendous difficulties with courage and strength. My Christian faith was important as a foundation for my work as a social worker; it provided me with the basic value that each person has infinite worth as a child created by God and is therefore worthy of respect and dignity, and free to make choices about how they want to live. I recognised that I was in no position to judge others, and I realised that in many cases all I could say was, 'There but for the grace of God, go I.' My role was not to judge, but to stand alongside as a fellow human being as clients tried to cope with the myriad of social and psychological problems integral to life in this imperfect world.

Yet, in appreciation of God's love and mercy towards me, I wanted to be more explicit and open about my Christian faith in my work with people, and therefore I applied to theological college for further training. As a result of this training, I was able to work as a hospital chaplain for one summer and then as a short-term missionary in southern Thailand the next summer.

When I was appointed as chaplain at a hospital for the mentally handicapped, I felt I had at last found my niche.

Each week, I led worship services and ran groups with stories, singing and crafts for residents on each floor, according to their level of functioning.

One morning, during my prayer time, I sensed God saying to me, 'I want you to be a minister.' Up until that point, I didn't think I could handle such a role, but I was open and willing to go in that direction if that was where God was leading me. Yet when I told some Christian friends what I thought God had said to me, they said that I must be mistaken – God didn't call *women* into the ministry. I felt hurt and uncertain; I didn't want to go against what I felt was God's will for me, yet I didn't want to push myself forward if I wasn't being backed by others in the church. In the end, I decided to set this vocation aside for a while, and instead to do some research into the issue of women in ministry during my second year at the theological college. Throughout the year I wavered in my sense of calling, believing in my heart that it was real and from God, but feeling uncertainty through my being a woman.

Regardless of what my final vocation was going to be, I found chaplaincy and mission work both fulfilling and enriching, and I considered them opportunities where I could in turn show something of God's love and concern to those who felt baffled by life's hardships and rejected by others. At the end of my second year of studies, I felt I ought to do further studies in social work, so I applied to the Master of Social Work programme at Carleton University in Ottawa. I was duly accepted.

All the while, I was learning to be content as a single person. From time to time, I did wonder if I might some day meet a Christian man who was sociable and fun, and who could accept my rebellious past, but I was grateful that God was honouring my commitment to follow him by opening up interesting opportunities for service and ministry. God was showing me that he could also look after my personal needs; following Jesus had become an adventure. I was no longer afraid of a future on my own. God would lead me in the right direction, and go with me step by step on my journey.

3

A Surprise Blessing

'"I tell you the truth," Jesus said to them, "no-one
who has left home or wife or brothers or parents or
children for the sake of the kingdom of God will
fail to receive many times as much in this age and,
in the age to come, eternal life"' (Luke 18:29–30)

Having been accepted into postgraduate studies in social
work at Carleton University, Ottawa, Canada's capital
city, one of my first tasks was to find myself somewhere
to live. This did not take long, and soon I had moved
into a rented property with four other Christian women
in similar circumstances to mine – postgraduate students
of one sort or another.

When Mary, a flatmate doing postgraduate studies in
geography, heard that I'd previously joined IVCF during
my undergraduate studies, she offered to take me along to
a Carleton VCF meeting. There she introduced me to the
student president, Mike, who was British. Mike had come
over from England to study perma-frost, and was in his
second year of a Masters of Arts degree in geography. He
was six feet tall, had long fair hair, and a reddish-blond
beard. His blue eyes twinkled with humour, and I was
instantly drawn to him. He knew he must look like a
renegade 'hippy', and apologised for his long hair –
explaining that he had just returned from a summer doing

research in the Yukon and hadn't yet had time to get it cut. He was friendly and welcoming, and had a clear crisp English accent. From the things he said, he was obviously intelligent and well read. Mike opened the meeting and introduced the staff worker, John Bowen, who was giving a brief welcoming talk to new and returning students.

As Mike gave the notices for the coming weeks, I watched him from the back of the room. He had a relaxed and easy-going manner that was very appealing. I felt strongly attracted to him, and wanted to get to know him more. I found my thoughts drifting as John Bowen was speaking, wondering whether Mike could possibly ever like me too. I surprised myself by even going so far as thinking that he was someone whom I would consider marrying. Lost in this fantasy, I was suddenly brought up short by John, who was sternly challenging students to be serious in their motives for coming to IVCF. 'You shouldn't be coming to IVCF in order to meet a boyfriend or girlfriend . . .' he was saying. I was duly chastened, but still incredibly attracted to Mike all the same!

Mike did seem to show an interest in me, and we chatted after the meeting. A few days later, we met again as Mary showed me around the geography reading room. 'Hello,' he said, 'Welcome to the "grad" room. How are you? You're on the Master of Social Work course, aren't you?' Mike then showed me his little corner: a simple white desk covered with papers he was obviously working on, and a bookshelf brimming with geography texts with photos of England hanging on any free space.

'That's right,' I replied. 'You have a nice reading room here – we don't have our own study areas in the social-work building. Ours is the small building at the other end of the campus. Beautiful pictures – where are they from?'

'Durham University – that's where I did my undergrad degree,' Mike replied.

I stared more closely at the photos. 'It's lovely – what an idyllic setting for a university. Actually, I've been near there. I have some cousins in Newcastle and a great aunt and uncle in Hexham, Allendale.'

'Oh, are your family from Britain, then?' Mike sounded interested.

'Yes, Mum is from Newcastle and Dad is from the Isle of Skye.'

'Hmm . . . Were you born there, too?' Mike asked.

'No, my parents met over here. I was born in Edmonton, Alberta, and I grew up in Toronto where my parents still live,' I answered.

We chatted on easily like this for what seemed ages, and then Mike suddenly said: 'Would you like to get together for lunch next week? Then I can let you know about the Carleton VCF.' We agreed to meet at the student cafeteria on the following Monday, and then Mary and I left.

On Monday, Mike and I met at the entrance of the cafeteria and he ushered me in. We found a seat for two, and after some everyday chit-chat, we talked about the Carleton IVCF group. 'We usually meet in a house over the road,' Mike began. 'First we meet together as a large group to have a light supper, and then we break into smaller Bible study groups for discussion.'

'I'm in the 'sports' group,' he continued. 'I play in the rugby team. Do you do any sports?'

'I didn't even know there was a rugby team here,' I replied. 'Yes – I used to be in the swimming team in high school, and I'd like to join here if I can.'

Mike smiled at me. 'Nancy is in it – I'll introduce you to her. She's leading our small group. Would you like to join us? I have to leave early next week, but I'll see you there.'

Lunch was soon over, and we each went off to our own classes. I found myself thinking about Mike a lot over the next week, and looking forward to the next IVCF meeting. The evening duly arrived, and I listened as Mike introduced the large group meeting and gave some general notices.

'We have a speaker from Toronto in town this week. He's the Ontario InterVarsity Christian Fellowship director, Don Posterski. He's speaking later tonight at the "Met" if anyone wants to leave early to hear him.'

We all went into different rooms as we broke into our smaller groups.

I knew Don Posterski because he attended my parents' church and I was interested in going to listen to him. Mike sat beside me as I joined in the small group for students also involved in sports on campus. After an hour or so, Mike turned to me and whispered that he had to leave; I assumed he was going to the meeting at the Met. I decided to go too. We slipped out together and walked down the stairs. At the door, we met another young woman and the three of us walked to the bus stop. We all hopped on to the bus and chatted away on the journey. At one point Mike turned to me and said, 'I will have to see if I can get you a ticket.' Don must be moving up in the world if one needed a ticket to hear him, I thought to myself, but I let the thought pass. We travelled into town and jumped off the bus.

Suddenly, I stopped dead in my tracks as I realised that we were heading for a large building in the centre of town. I had no idea where the 'Met' was, but I did recognise that *this* was the National Arts Centre. Mike and the other girl were behind me and crashed into me as I came to an abrupt halt. An awful thought was slowly dawning on me, and I turned to Mike with a question on my lips. 'We are going to hear Don, aren't we?'

Mike brushed past and replied, 'No, we're going to see a ballet. Hurry up if you want to come, because we're already late.'

I stood in bewilderment for a moment, and then quickly followed them in. 'Are you sure you don't mind me coming along, I mean . . .' Mike bought me a ticket and we ran to our seats.

As far as I was concerned, it was a dreadful modern production – totally incomprehensible and obscure. I was also feeling acutely embarrassed that I had inadvertently barged in on their outing. I was still feeling very uncomfortable when the ballet ended and we all walked to a nearby pub for a drink. To try to hide my embarrassment, I talked non-stop. At the end of the evening we hopped on a bus to go home and the other girl jumped off at her stop, which was before ours. Mike walked me to the second stop where I had to change buses, and we chatted along the way. Finally, I plucked up enough courage to say, 'Mike, I don't really know what to say, but did I barge in on your date? I'm really sorry.'

Mike threw his head back and laughed. 'No, she invited herself too, because I had some free tickets – one of my flatmates helped to produce the ballet.' He turned to me with a smile and said, 'It was pretty awful, wasn't it? I liked having you along; you helped to keep the conversation going.' I was feeling really embarrassed by the time I got home. I knew that I liked Mike very much, but felt I had probably made a complete fool of myself. Yet I comforted myself with the thought that if he was still interested in me, he would at least know from the beginning that I could be quite scatterbrained!

Over the next few weeks, Mike did ring to invite me, Mary and another of my flatmates, Joanne, out to various places. The four of us had some very happy times together – cycling, going to the cinema, and preparing breakfast on an open fire in a wood in the nearby Gatineau hills. It was beautiful there as the leaves were starting to turn brilliant crimson and gold. By this time, I knew that I was thoroughly besotted with Mike, but I feared that he just wanted to be friends. This thought was also voiced by my flatmates, who warned me that Mike was just a friendly bloke who had many girls who liked him.

It concerned me that I might be reverting to my silly teenage years, and I was determined not to spend my postgraduate years wasting emotional energy by dreaming about a possible relationship that was not going to happen. One evening I went for a walk on my own to talk it out with God. I wandered down by a little waterfall at the back of our lane, and I listened to the rushing water as I walked beside the river. 'God, you know that I like Mike, but I promised you I would follow Jesus first. If it's your will, I pray that you will lead us together, but I don't want to waste my time dreaming about him. I leave it in your hands.'

I drew my jacket around me as I walked briskly back home. It was getting cold and the autumn air blew through my light jacket, but I felt warm in my heart for I knew that I no longer needed to worry about my relationship with Mike. God would look after the situation. As far as I was concerned, the next move had to be Mike's. If he wanted to contact me he could, but I was going to concentrate on my studies.

To my surprise and delight, Mike phoned me the next evening and asked me out to a concert the following Saturday evening. This time it was to be just Mike and I – there were no flatmates to accompany us. I felt totally ecstatic, and had to restrain myself from doing cartwheels across our sitting-room floor.

By a strange coincidence, I also got a phone call from another interesting young man that evening. It was Bruce – a friend of another of the girls I shared the house with. Bruce was handsome, intelligent and witty, and was also ringing to ask me out! I thanked him for asking, but declined, explaining that I had already agreed to go out with Mike. I couldn't help thinking that it never rains but it pours!

The following Saturday evening marked the official beginning of my courtship with Mike. Although I arrived just as the concert was beginning, having caught two buses to get there, Mike was still waiting by the doors – albeit a little uncertainly, obviously wondering if I was going to turn up. We ran in just as the music was starting up. The concert was lovely, although rather long, and I found myself becoming sleepy. Once it was over, though, and we were back outside, the fresh air revived me. We crossed the road to a little pub for a drink and a bite to eat.

We talked about our respective childhoods, Mike's in England and mine in Canada with British parents. We marvelled at our similar interests and values, and our mutual appreciation of socialising, music and sport. The light was dim in the pub, but as we looked into each other's eyes we knew that there was something special between us. As we waited outside for the bus to take us home, Mike gently kissed me. His English tweed cap knocked off my woollen Tam o' Shanter, and we laughed as we both stooped to pick it up.

From that moment on, Mike and I were inseparable. We got together during class breaks, and I often joined him in his reading room where we would both study. We often had lunch together and sometimes we would invite each other round for an evening meal. I watched him play rugby and we went cycling and hiking together. It soon became obvious to our respective classmates and also to the students in the IVCF group that we were a couple. We started going to church together and enjoyed the spiritual fellowship of worshipping with each other.

As the winter closed in and the snow fell in heaps, we changed from cycling to skiing and went cross-country skiing each Saturday with other students. We set off for the whole day, taking a rucksack of food on our backs, stopping only once for lunch. The fresh air was bracing and the exercise stimulating. Gradually we became more proficient until we were brave enough to tackle the steep 'expert' hills. We both loved the outdoors and the feeling of being physically tired at the end of the day, when we would return home for a hot meal and sip steaming cups of coffee as we played Scrabble and card games with friends. On weekday evenings we often went skating on the canal – Ottawa boasted the longest skating rink in the world.

On a few occasions Mike invited a group of friends and we all went away for a weekend of downhill skiing. I always marvelled at what a good organiser Mike was, and really appreciated his sociability. With Mike there, there was bound to be much laughter, banter and fun. Many of our skiing friends were also university students, but many were not Christians. Yet we all had friendly discussions about God and Christianity, and I could see that everyone respected Mike for his beliefs. He demonstrated that being a Christian could be both exciting and fun. Mike had integrity of faith, while still having an open and enquiring mind. He had a wholesome lifestyle, but one that was rich and full. I was proud to be associated with him, and pleased that together we could be a Christian witness to others.

At Christmas, Mike came to my parents' home in Toronto to meet my family. Immediately, he was accepted by everyone as one of the family. Everybody appreciated his open and friendly manner. The rest of that university year flew by, for we were always so busy – with our studies, IVCF, part-time jobs and just spending time together. Basically, we shared each other's lives: whether we were studying or reading for pleasure, enjoying outdoor sport or discussion groups, listening to music, or worshipping together. Gradually we grew closer and closer and our friendship and love for each other grew.

I told Mike of my rebellious past and my previous relationships. Mike was compassionate and understanding. He brushed it all aside, and reassured me that if God had forgiven me, then I was forgiven, and the past was forgotten. I was deeply grateful for his unconditional acceptance and marvelled afresh at God's generous grace.

The university summer term ended all too quickly, and I knew that Mike was planning to go home to England for the entire summer holidays – from May to August. It felt like a terrible wrench to part, but I was somehow brave and cheerful when the moment came for him to leave, having caught something of his excitement and anticipation at going home. I also knew that I was going to see him in a couple of months, when I too would be going to England to meet Mike's parents. I didn't have much time to mope around as I was writing my major research paper during the day and working at my part-time job in emergency housing in the evenings.

I tried to write to Mike every day, usually pouring out my thoughts and feelings in the evenings when I was working at the hostel and the residents had gone to bed. He, in turn, wrote less frequently, and I occasionally had pangs of uncertainty about our relationship.

One evening as I cycled home from work, after not hearing from him for about three weeks, I pondered on his uncharacteristic silence, and wondered if he was becoming unsure of his feelings for me. I peddled hard on the last stretch home and looked up at the stars ahead of me as I glided down the hill. God seemed near and I admitted to him my feelings of insecurity. In an inaudible voice, I heard God say to me, 'You will marry Mike.'

'Really?' I asked in surprise. It was as if I could see God smile a broad smile and say, 'Do you not think that I can bless you in this way?'

'Oh!' was all I could reply. It dawned on me that

somewhere in my unconscious I assumed that God was punishing me for my rebellious youth by keeping me single. And I still did not believe that God had completely forgiven me. In my imagination, sometimes God seemed to be a hard taskmaster, constantly correcting me and preventing me from having fun. Deep down, though, I knew that God wanted my trust, not in order to restrict me and restrain me but instead to bless me and use me. Joy filled my heart as I marvelled at his undeserved favour. My doubts and uncertainty disappeared. The following day, three letters from Mike arrived in the post – he'd written every week, but the letters had been held up in transit.

August soon arrived and Mike met me at Heathrow airport after my overnight flight. He was his same old self, warm and fun-loving. I felt a little nervous meeting his parents for the first time, but they were very welcoming and helped me to feel at home. England completely captivated me, with its ancient castles and historical buildings, little villages with pubs, and all the surrounding fields of sheep.

As we drove around the countryside, I marvelled at the gentle rolling green hills. In Canada, the fields had usually turned somewhat brown by August after the long hot summer sun. But here they remained a soft green. I was also thrilled with the bright scarlet poppies scattered throughout the fields and often clustered by the roadside. Poppies do not grow wild in Canada – perhaps because the weather is too extreme. The enchanting poppies were a happy sight, and seemed to reflect my inner happiness as Mike and I enjoyed our outings in England.

We packed lots of activity into our holiday. We attended outdoor plays, and visited family and friends. I felt that Mike's parents warmed to me, and his sister, Maggie, was great fun. We spent many hours swimming in the sea on the south-east coast and flying kites on the

lush grass above the beaches at Margate. We arrived back
in Canada at the end of the summer looking suntanned
and healthy, with our hair bleached by the sun. It had
been such exceptional weather – our friends in Canada
hardly believed that we had been in England!

After such a joyous holiday together, I was confused
when Mike seemed to be distancing himself a little from
me when we returned to our university studies. He was
very busy writing his thesis, so I didn't see him quite
so much, and when he had some free time he seemed
to prefer to spend time with other friends. It was such a
contrast to the closeness we had enjoyed on our visit to
England that I wondered if he was having doubts about
our relationship. By this time, I was deeply in love with
Mike, and hoped that we would get married. We had
never talked about marriage, but we both knew we had
a growing commitment to one another. Our relationship
had developed so gradually and naturally – we were
always comfortable with one another. My doubts were
not helped, though, when my flatmate said that she also
had noticed a change in Mike's behaviour towards me.
She also voiced her concern that Mike might be 'using'
me – a viewpoint that both shocked and hurt me.

Eventually Mike noticed that something was troubling
me, so we met at a pub one evening to talk. We sat down
at a small round table, ordered drinks, and then Mike
said, 'You seem unusually quiet these days – what's
bothering you?'

'I may be wrong,' I said hesitantly, 'but after we had
such a wonderful time in England, it feels as if you
are "backing off" a little. Is this true? Or am I just
imagining things?'

Mike looked thoughtfully down at his beer and slowly
took a sip. He didn't say anything, so I expanded on what
I had said. 'My flatmate thinks you are using me. I don't
think that – at least, I haven't thought that – but it makes

me wonder about things when you keep saying that you want to go back to England when you've finished your studies.' Slowly, I found the courage to voice the rest of my fears. 'I guess I'm scared that after a wonderful year and a half together, you're going to go back to England next spring and leave me.'

Without responding directly to what I had said, Mike suggested that we go for a walk, so we finished our drinks and wandered down the pathway beside the canal. It was getting dark, but the evening was still warm and there was a light breeze blowing back my hair as we strolled side by side. We came upon a bench and Mike suggested that we sit down for a while. By this time, I was lost in my unhappy thoughts, fearing that he wanted to break off our relationship, when Mike suddenly blurted out, 'Will you marry me – even though I fart in bed?'

I was so stunned that I didn't know whether to laugh or cry. If the proposal was somewhat unconventional, then so was my acceptance of it: 'Yes – so long as you don't pull the bedclothes over my head!' I burst into fits of laughter through my tears, hardly able to believe that Mike had really proposed to me.

Suddenly, Mike became very serious. 'Catherine, I've been thinking of asking you to marry me for many months, but I needed to be absolutely sure before I asked you. I am sure now. You know that I love you – I can't imagine my life without you.' He looked down at me with a gentle smile and we kissed.

We decided to keep our engagement to ourselves until we had a chance to tell our respective parents. We wanted to tell my parents in person three weeks later when we would be visiting them for Thanksgiving weekend. I went home hugging this incredibly happy secret to myself, my heart brimming with love.

In contrast to my previous engagement to Mark, this time I was happy and excited. In fact, I had real difficulty in keeping it secret for the next three weeks because I was beaming with joy. There was a permanent smile on my face. My flatmates noticed my excessive cheerfulness, and when we eventually told them, they said they had suspected as much.

We did manage to keep the secret, though, and in due course we told my parents of our engagement. I hoped it wouldn't be too much for them, as two of my brothers had recently got engaged too. My parents were not surprised at our news, but definitely delighted, and gave us a lovely tablecloth as an engagement present. It had taken Mike the entire Thanksgiving weekend to pluck up enough courage to speak to my parents – and by the Sunday afternoon I began to wonder if he was ever going to say anything! It then dawned on me that he was actually nervous – it was so unlike him that I teased him a little in private. In the end we told my parents together – recognising that the days when a prospective suitor had to ask a lady's father for her 'hand' were long past. We immediately telephoned England and let Mike's family know our happy news. All our family and friends were pleased and happy for us. By this time, I was wearing the dainty diamond cluster ring that Mike had given me.

We decided to set the wedding date for the following summer, so that we could both finish our studies, and so that our family and friends would be on holiday and able to celebrate this special day with us. It would be quite a summer for my family, as my brothers were planning their weddings near then too! My youngest brother, David, was to marry his fiancée Robin in June; Mike and I chose August; and my middle brother, Iain, and his fiancée, Judy, picked September.

It was hard waiting nearly a whole year till we would be together as husband and wife, but we were both busy finishing our Master's degrees and working part time – I as a counsellor at the emergency hostel, and

Mike as teaching assistant in the geography department
of the university. Despite our work commitments, we
managed to continue to enjoy sports and outings together
– cycling, skiing, skating and hiking. We also kept up
our involvement with the IVCF group on campus. We
were now in different small groups, and I started a
one-to-one Bible study with Margo, one of the girls in
my small group.

Margo was attractive and athletic. She was tall and
stocky, whereas I was petite and small-boned. We had
been in the small 'sports' group together and had become
friends. I knew that she had liked Mike at one time, so at
first I was a little hesitant to tell her of our engagement.
I need not have worried – she was extremely gracious
and expressed happiness for us. Margo and I continued
studying the Book of Romans together. One day we came
to a verse where the apostle Paul gives encouragement to
the believers in Rome who, in his day, were experiencing
persecution for their faith. Paul reminded them that Jesus
was with them and would never leave them:

> For I am convinced that neither death nor life,
> neither angels nor demons, neither the present nor
> the future, nor any powers, neither height nor depth,
> nor anything else in all creation, will be able to
> separate us from the love of God that is in Christ
> Jesus our Lord (Romans 8:38–9).

I thought about this verse, then said to Margo, 'This
means that even if, God forbid, Mike ever died, I would
still be OK because my first allegiance is to God, and I
know he would still love me and remain with me.' Margo
and I then spent some time thinking about God's love for
us, and hoped that we would have such faith if either of
us found ourselves in that situation.

After spending Christmas with my parents, Mike and I,

and Margo, along with thirty or so other Carleton VCF students, travelled down to Urbana, Illinois, for an IVCF mission conference. It was an inspiring and challenging experience, where we were all able to focus our attention on our futures and consider where we were to go and what we were to do. We believed that God wanted us to serve him by serving other people. We all returned home humbled and determined to follow God more sincerely in all areas of our lives. For Mike and I, this included our struggle with the tension of our physical attraction towards one another. At this point, we reaffirmed our decision to wait until we were married before having sex.

Mike finished off his thesis and continued to work as a research assistant in the geography department, while also remaining involved in the IVCF group. I was still completing my studies, and started working full time with the local social services in income support. We happily planned for and anticipated our wedding, but we were not sure where we should live once we were married. Mike applied for all sorts of jobs in geography in England and failed to find anything; nor could he find any geography positions in Canada because he only had a student visa. He was beginning to feel very discouraged when John Bowen, who was aware of his job search, asked him if he would be interested in taking a part-time job as staff intern with IVCF at Ottawa University. At the same time, Mike was also offered a part-time teaching post in the geography department at Carleton University. In the end, he decided to do both jobs for the coming year.

Our August wedding day finally arrived, and we had a very happy celebration with our family and friends in attendance. The sun blazed its brilliance and God seemed to be smiling on us. We were pleased that so many of Mike's family and friends could come over from England for the wedding. It was a traditional wedding in which I wore a full-length Laura Ashley gown, and Mike wore top hat and tails. We made our vows in deep sincerity, and enjoyed the joyous reception afterwards which was held at another local church. After a relaxing honeymoon at my grandparents' cottage, when we swam in the fresh water of Georgian Bay, played tennis and did some sightseeing, we settled into a small flat on the top floor of a house back in Ottawa.

Life was fun and exciting as we kept up our friendships and sports activities, along with our involvement with IVCF, work and church. I completed my major research paper just before Christmas, and we had a special Christmas in England visiting Mike's parents. We found that we both really enjoyed the companionship of married life – sharing our lives emotionally, socially, physically and spiritually. My job as welfare worker was interesting, but I kept hoping to find a job that entailed more direct use of my counselling skills. Mike was once again faced with looking for a full-time job when the university year ended in May. We wondered where God would lead us.

Mike again applied for many geography posts in both England and Canada, but to no avail. In the meantime, he was offered a full-time position with IVCF at McMaster University in Hamilton. It was a difficult decision for him to give up his geography, after completing his Master's degree, and finding it both interesting and rewarding; he was aware that it would be very difficult for him to return to the field some years later, if he did not first gain some work experience after graduation.

There was also the consideration of salary. Many of his friends had starting positions at the equivalent rate of about £15,000–£20,000. As a staff worker with IVCF, his annual salary would only amount to about the equivalent of £4,000. We prayed together as Mike seriously considered his purpose and calling. He acknowledged that he didn't want his primary concern to be making money; he wanted to serve God. Mike compared the two different careers and decided that it was more important – from a Christian perspective – to serve people, and to attempt to play at least some small part in extending God's Kingdom. Thus he chose to accept the job as IVCF staff worker at McMaster University.

God seemed to confirm our decision, as I too was quickly able to find a job in Hamilton, as a medical social worker in a hospital where my best friend, Julie, already worked. We found a little house to rent, just across the road from the university, and happily settled into our new life in this 'steel town' of Ontario.

I found my new job as medical social worker very enriching, for I visited the new mothers in the maternity ward. It gave me many opportunities to develop my counselling and reporting skills, and also to build up my judgement-ability in psycho/social and family assessments. It was a very challenging post, as there were ten stillbirths in the first couple of months that I worked there. I quickly had to learn about grief counselling, and began to see how the parents involved found it beneficial to talk about their experiences of loss. Many parents found it very helpful to see and hold their stillborn baby, in order for them to begin the grieving process.

Meanwhile, Mike plunged wholeheartedly into his work, and enjoyed it to the hilt. He understood university life, and, having served as a former IVCF student president and also as a staff intern, had good training and experience to enable him to understand his facilitating role. Mike naturally took the initiative and loved to help in the planning of activities and events. He encouraged the students as they led weekly small groups and the large group meeting that was held once a month. Because of his many qualities, Mike easily formed warm and caring relationships with the students and spent time with many on an individual basis.

It was rewarding for me to take part in his work in a secondary way, by serving on the Area Support Committee. We enjoyed the friendship and fellowship of the network of former IVCF students and adult supporters. Frequently, students came over to our home for planning meetings and we enjoyed each other's company over a meal.

Mike's work extended in the following year as he was given the added responsibility of Brock University in St Catharines, a town nearby, and was also given the position of area director of this south-west area of Ontario. His job now included attendance at annual conferences and a leadership role at Ontario Pioneer Camps, the IVCF summer camp. Mike was a natural witness to all students with his easy-going manner. He showed that being a Christian could be fun and fulfilling, and through his example many were drawn to consider following Jesus. We also settled into a local church and began to build friendships with neighbours.

Our joy was made complete when we discovered that I was expecting a baby. It was at this point that we used all our savings and borrowed some money from my father to raise the deposit to buy a property. We bought a semi-detached house up on the Hamilton 'mountain' (part of the Niagara escarpment) and moved in just a fortnight before the baby was due. We hurried to decorate the nursery, and settled in just in time for the arrival of our son, James, on 16 November 1987. I then had an extended maternity leave of nine months. I found the weeks at home following James's birth very hectic and tiring, but we were extremely happy. God seemed to be watching over us and blessing us.

Late one afternoon, as we were driving home to Hamilton from Toronto, we had to stop the car halfway up the steep escarpment because our car had a flat tyre; James was crying because he was hungry for his supper. We felt helpless being in such an awkward place where there were no phones for a mile or so either way. Eventually, a car saw our plight and stopped to offer help. A swarthy, Spanish-looking man climbed out of his vehicle, and when we explained that we weren't too far from home, he offered to drive James and me to the house so we could telephone the Automobile Association. Meanwhile, Mike was to stay by the car to wait for help. Before we had had time to think about all this, the man had shuffled James and me into his car, and we were gone. Mike was left standing there, suddenly realising that he had just let his wife and newborn son go off with a strange man. There was little he could do, so he prayed, 'Lord, I trust them to you.' Shortly afterwards, a police car pulled up and the officer helped Mike to change the tyre and he arrived home safely. We were both grateful that God had protected us, and we renewed our commitment of our lives to his keeping.

We were basking in the joy of God's care and his many blessings in our fulfilling jobs and beautiful son. Life seemed to be falling into place; Mike's ministry to students was developing; the IVCF group at McMaster University had grown from forty to eighty students in the two years Mike had been leading it. He never looked back with regret on his decision to set aside his geography, and his commitment to IVCF work grew still further as he developed in his role. We enjoyed many close friendships and felt settled in the community. The local church was caring, and we felt a sense of belonging there. The future seemed to be laid out promisingly before us – until Mike's sudden death.

4

Valley of Grief

'Who has understood the mind of the Lord, or instructed him as his counsellor?' (Isaiah 40:13.)

After a fitful night of tossing and turning as my mind went round and round trying to absorb the news that my husband was dead, I woke the next morning feeling as if I hadn't slept a wink. My head was pounding and my eyes were puffy and red. My heart was heavy and my mood utterly depressed. I awoke with the awareness of the stark fact that Mike was gone, and was never coming back. I thought about how special he was and how well we got on, how I would miss his ability to plan, to take the initiative, his sense of adventure, his enjoyment of sport and good music, his friendliness and sociability. I just kept thinking, 'How will I be able to go on without him? Life will be so bleak.' Tears welled up again as the sorrow threatened to overwhelm me. Silently, I prayed, 'Oh God, I already miss him so much. Why did I have to be left behind – why couldn't you have taken me too?'

Then I heard the sound of a baby's cry from another room and I was suddenly reminded that I had to take care of James. I had to go on for him. I dragged myself out of bed to wash and dress, wondering if I would ever stop crying, and if my eyes would ever stop stinging. I struggled to swallow some breakfast and fed James; my mother had already got him changed and dressed. I sat in the sitting-room in a daze while feeding him. Soon, other members of my family arrived. My middle brother, Iain, and Judy, his wife, had arrived earlier that morning. David and Robin, my youngest brother and his wife, then arrived from London, in Ontario. Having got married in the same year, we also had our first babies at the same time – David's and Robin's son, Ben, was only six days older than James. David and Robin both hugged me, as did Iain, and said how shocked and sad they were to hear of Mike's death. Much as everyone wanted to help, they all knew that there was little that could be said to ease my pain.

Being a practical person, David asked me about my financial situation. He asked me whether we'd had insurance on our mortgage and our car loan. I hadn't even thought about all this yet. It now hit me that one of the implications of Mike's death was that I was now the sole financial provider. I realised that I didn't even know what insurance policies we had, so he phoned my best friend Julie MacDonald, from my parents' church in Toronto, now in Hamilton, and asked her to go over to our house to see what documents she could find.

Later that afternoon, Julie and her husband arrived from Hamilton. We cried together and she said how terribly sorry she was, and how people at work were all thinking of me. They brought along all the important documents I'd need. As they left, she turned back and hesitantly asked me a question. 'Catherine, I hate to ask you this, but do you want us to bring some clothes for Mike?' I cringed inside as the stark reality that he was dead penetrated a little further at this practical detail.

'Yes, I guess so. I suppose his jeans and ski-suit aren't particularly suitable for the funeral, and who knows what kind of state they are in.'

Julie asked gently, 'What would you like us to fetch? Is there a particular suit or something you would like?'

I took a deep breath before replying. 'Well, he only owns one suit. It's dark grey – it's in the cupboard.'

'OK, we'll find it,' Julie continued, 'and a shirt and tie. Is this all right with you?'

'Yes. Yes. Thank you,' I managed to reply.

As she left, I thought about the last time Mike had worn his suit. We had been going out to an evening service at which he was speaking. Just as we were about to leave, he approached me with his suit trousers dangling from his arm. 'Oh, Catherine, I've caught the hem on my shoe – could you sew it up?' In a rush I replied, 'We're late already – here, how about taping it up with some masking tape for now, and I'll sew it later.' As I remembered this, I felt embarrassed to think that I never did sew up his left trouser leg. And now he was going to be buried in trousers hemmed with masking tape. I pushed this ludicrous thought out of my mind – I couldn't deal with it just now.

I looked through the financial papers and documents that Julie and her husband had brought with them, and quickly spotted the fact that we had not taken out mortgage insurance. Some of the practical difficulties I was going to have to face began to dawn on me. I wondered aloud at some of the possible implications. 'Will I have to sell the house? We only bought it a couple of months ago. Will I have to go back to work right away? Will James not even have a mummy to look after him either?' Once again, tears pricked my eyes. Before I could become totally despondent and filled with self-pity, my brother Iain stopped me. 'Try not to worry about that side of things – I'm sure we'll be able to sort something out. We'll help you to work out what to do.'

Over the next couple of days, friends kept dropping in and just sitting and talking. I was deeply touched by their love and concern. Through my haze of grief, I greeted those people from my parents' church who called in. As

I walked around the house in a stupor, I noticed flowers appearing everywhere. I thought to myself, 'This house is beginning to look like a funeral parlour,' then it suddenly dawned on me that the flowers *were* for a funeral – Mike's funeral.

My former pastor, Dr Baxter, visited me and I burst into tears as he held my hand in sympathy. He said simply and gently, 'He's in God's hands now.'

'I know, but I miss him so much!' I sobbed.

'We're with you, Catherine, and God is with you.' I found his strength and wisdom comforting, and I was happy to lean on him.

The telephone then rang and I went to answer it. It was a friend from theological college whom I hadn't seen for years. She was surprised to get me on my parents' phone. 'Oh Catherine, is that you? I heard something on the radio about a terrible accident . . .' I confirmed that it was Mike who had died. She said she was so very sorry, and asked me about the funeral arrangements. It was a terrible strain to remain emotionally intact when dealing with such calls, especially as not everyone who telephoned knew the situation.

Shortly after this, my grandparents arrived from Ottawa, along with my wheelchair-bound uncle who was suffering from multiple sclerosis. My grandfather had come from Newcastle upon Tyne and had loved Mike, being a fellow Englishman and fellow graduate of Durham University, right from their very first meeting. Grandad just held me tight, and together we sobbed as we acknowledged our sorrow and sadness at Mike's death.

My sister, Fiona, and her husband and their son then arrived from Alabama. Fiona came to me in tears and put her arms around me. 'Oh Catherine, I'm just so sorry that this has happened to you.' We then cried on each other's shoulders, knowing that there was little else to be said.

Church friends were very helpful and brought some

meals to help with all the guests. Once again, I felt amazed at the love and care of my family and, amid my pain, felt a certain comfort. One particular Bible verse came to mind: 'Religion that God our Father accepts as pure and faultless is this: to look after orphans and widows in their distress . . .' (James 1:27). I did feel wrapped up and held close in the warm blanket of their love. God was replacing Mike's love for me, by love from my family and the family of God. I didn't doubt that God still loved me – even though I couldn't understand how he could have let this happen – because his love was being poured out in such abundant measure in my family and friends.

My parents came with me to see the funeral director. As I drove along, I looked up at the blue sky and wondered how life could carry on as if nothing had changed, when my whole world had collapsed. It seemed as if there should at least be a couple of seconds of silence in respect, but the sky was blue, and people were rushing here and there with their daily tasks. I wanted to scream out, 'But my husband is dead! Don't you know? My husband is dead!'

I walked with my parents into the funeral director's office. It was like a very grand hotel, with attendants walking silently and discreetly past. The carpet was plush and the offices were wood-panelled. Everything seemed so controlled and tidy. Cushioned settees with highly polished tables and ornate lamps decorated the rooms.

The funeral director wore a sombre expression and had a sympathetic manner. He spoke in a hushed tone, almost as a parent might to a young child in a church service – wanting to make sure that the child doesn't misbehave, yet not wanting to create a scene in public. In a detached, professional manner he enquired what date we would prefer to have the funeral. We agreed to have it on Thursday, for it would take that long for the body to be transferred from the Grey Bruce Hospital, and to be 'attended to'. He suggested we put a notice in the local newspapers giving the time and date of the funeral. He set out the wording in a repetitive and formal way, but none of us was able to think clearly enough to amend it to be more personal.

Then came the decision of what coffin to choose. The funeral director asked me to follow him into the back room, where I was to pick one that I thought was appropriate. It was like going from the waiting-room into a dentist's office behind closed doors, and a sense of unreality set in as I looked at one after another of the ornate, gilded coffins. They were polished wood and marble with heavy brass handles, and their excessive grandeur repulsed me. Each was filled with fluffy satin pillows and frilly sheets. Bouquets of fresh flowers overpowered the room with their sickly-sweet fragrance.

I thought how ridiculous it was to have a dead body lying on sheets and pillows as if the person were just asleep, when really they were dead. I certainly didn't want any sort of farcical set-up. Nor did I think it was appropriate to spend such a lot of money on something that was just going to rot under ground. It was all just show.

In my disgust with the artificiality and the assumed solemnity of the entire scene, I was rather blunt in my considerations. 'What's the cheapest you've got?' I asked.

The funeral director looked a little surprised. 'Oh, this grey one, made of a strengthened cardboard,' he answered.

'That is what I would like,' I said, and turned around and walked back into the other room.

I think the funeral director was appalled by my apparent 'lack of respect' for the dead, and I don't think he had any understanding of how I felt. However, I was so firm that he went straight ahead with my order. Having to pick out a coffin forced me afresh to face the fact that Mike was actually dead, but the euphemisms used, and the elaborate surroundings of the funeral parlour, only seemed to try to deny this reality.

My parents seemed to understand how I felt and did not question my wishes; however, my father approached me later, at home, and said gently, 'Catherine, I understand that you do not want an overly elaborate coffin, which just wouldn't have been Mike, but don't you think that the cardboard coffin that you chose might be misunderstood? Some people associate a cardboard coffin with a pauper's grave.'

'Oh, I hadn't thought about that at all,' I replied. This was all so new to me that I had no idea of how people would view my choice. In the end, my father offered to go back and choose something simple in wood, and I agreed that this would be better.

My father also suggested that we didn't have people come to visit us at the funeral parlour, the normal Canadian custom, but instead invite people to come over to my parents' house if they wanted to pay their respects. I was grateful for this suggestion – I had no desire to stand beside even a closed coffin with Mike's body in it, while people walked by feeling uncomfortable and mouthing meaningless platitudes. It did seem more personal for people to come to my parents' home. After all, we did believe that Mike was no longer with us – his body was in reality just his remains. We were the ones needing comfort; we were the ones left behind. I was grateful to my parents for their generous hospitality, especially as there would be so many coming. Judy and Iain helped by tidying up and cleaning; and some people from the church brought over some casseroles to help with the large number of people needing to be fed.

My sister Fiona and my sister-in-law Robin helped to look after James while I was busy talking to people and making decisions about the funeral plans. In the middle of the afternoon, Robin brought James to me, looking content and peaceful. As I thanked her, she explained, 'I have just fed him. He wouldn't take a bottle, so in the end I breastfed him myself.' I was amazed. My own wet nurse! It was so thoughtful and kind and generous. She also offered to let me breastfeed Ben, who was always hungry, because I myself had too much milk. It was odd swapping babies, yet it was such a help that I could only marvel at this strange but helpful provision.

Later, when we both went up to the bedroom to feed our own babies, I told her of how Mike had tried to feed James once – was it really only a fortnight ago? So much had happened that it felt like a lifetime ago. 'I went out to the shops and was a little late coming home. When I got home, James was howling his little head off, and Mike was desperately trying to pacify him with a bottle of sugar water. He had carefully read the baby book to check how to do it. At that point, we had no milk formula and he didn't know what to give him. Mike was so proud to be a father. He was so helpful; he wasn't afraid to change nappies – in fact, he even bathed James before I did! Also, when I was totally exhausted and having to get up twice in the night to feed James in the first few weeks, Mike fetched him for me and laid him down beside me so that I barely had to wake up to feed him, and then he would change him and put him back in his cot.' I wept as I remembered Mike's kindness. Yet again it hit me that from now on I would have the total responsibility of raising and caring for James. Robin was so kind to me; she was not just a sister-in-law, but a sister-in-Christ.

Yet in the midst of my grief, I was experiencing God's grace. It was a mystery I couldn't fully comprehend. I was bearing up much better than I ever thought I could – God seemed to be giving me his supernatural strength.

It reminded me of the wise words that Corrie ten Boom's father said to her when she worried about getting caught for hiding Jews during the Second World War:

> 'Corrie,' he began gently, 'when you and I go to Amsterdam – when do I give you your ticket?' I sniffed a few times, considering this. 'Why, just before we get on the train.' 'Exactly. And our wise Father in heaven knows when we're going to need things, too. Don't run out ahead of him, Corrie. When the time comes that some of us will have to die, you will look into your heart and find the strength you need – just in time.'[1]

I remembered the time when I was pregnant and I had thought to myself, whatever would happen if Mike died? How could I go on? I felt that I couldn't. I recalled one pregnant woman in hospital who had lost her husband in a car accident the week before. As a social worker on the maternity ward, I was asked to visit her. But I really didn't want to – I was seven months' pregnant myself and the situation was just too close for comfort. I delayed going to see her, hoping that somehow I could avoid it. However, a nurse asked me again and we started to discuss her situation. Tears came to our eyes as we tried to imagine how hard it must be for her. 'I think it helps to have faith in God – to know that he would always be with you, so that you'd never be totally alone,' I said.

Soon after, another nurse approached us and said, 'Catherine, it's OK, she doesn't want you to see her – she's got her priest and her family with her, and she doesn't want to see a stranger.' I sighed with relief.

Was God preparing me in that incident? I don't know. Whenever I had such morbid thoughts, I would quickly dismiss them from my mind, never thinking it could ever happen to me. But here I was, just a few months later, in a similar situation. Would my faith see me through? Or, more accurately, would God really help me through this overpowering grief? Would he be able to heal this gaping hole? Amazingly, he was helping so far, but it still hurt so much and I felt so weak and weary.

My pastor and his wife arrived from Hamilton; and Don Posterski, Mike's boss with IVCF, also came over. Don greeted me with his usual playful greeting, 'Lady Catherine, I loved Mike. We were all so shocked by this accident. All the students are reeling, but they are bearing up. They wanted me to tell you that they are specially praying for you.'

On the practical issues, Don gave me some encouraging news: IVCF was setting up a benevolent fund for James and me, and a trust fund for James's education. Family were also very generous in giving financial help to pay for the funeral and burial. It was yet another way in which God was meeting our needs through his people. I was deeply touched, but also a little embarrassed. I found it hard to accept such gifts – I had always been taught that it is more blessed to give than to receive. For James's sake, though, I decided to accept – graciously, I hope.

The various ministers pressed me to make some decisions about what I wanted for a funeral service. Don asked me if I wanted the service to be held in Hamilton or Toronto.

'I don't know. I haven't even thought about it,' I replied. There seemed to be so much to think about. Dr Baxter came to the rescue and suggested, 'Why don't you have two services? You could have a funeral service here in Toronto, and a memorial service in Hamilton.' I marvelled at this simple, yet creative, solution and was relieved to have the decision made for me.

Yet I was also pleased to be consulted and invited to have input in deciding what type of service to hold. It felt more personal and more meaningful, and forced me to face the reality of Mike's death. But I found it all very difficult. I kept saying, 'I don't know what to include – I've never even *been* to a funeral before!' Don was encouraging and said, 'Catherine, we're here for you, and we'll all help you in the planning of the services.'

'Thank you,' I said. 'All I know is that I want the services to be proper and right, and most of all to be real.'

'Don't you worry, we understand how you feel,' Don said gently.

We picked some music, and Fiona thought of a hymn that Mike and I had chosen for our wedding, just two and a half years ago at my parents' church in Toronto. Dr Baxter said that he thought it would be appropriate to have a private family interment at the grave-side after the service, and I agreed.

I was really grateful to have these pastors to lean on for support, men whom I could trust to prepare a service that would be fitting for the circumstances and that would appropriately remember Mike as he was. It seemed incredible to be sitting in my parents' sitting-room planning a funeral for my husband, who was only twenty-seven years old. He was two years younger than me, a fact that never bothered me as he was so mature and responsible, yet still able to have fun. What did I have to look forward to now that he was gone?

Every morning when I woke up, the heavy feeling would be there. The depression and loneliness descended like a grey and suffocating blanket. I felt a deep ache, a gaping hole. I missed him so much. I knew I'd never feel his arms around me, we'd never kiss, never make love again. It was so final. 'Why, God? Why? How could you allow this to happen?' Around and around, my mind would try to comprehend the incomprehensible.

It was my custom to read a passage of Scripture in the morning, so I flipped to the day's verses as listed in my Scripture Union notes. In the commotion of the previous few days, I hadn't done my readings, but my need was so great that I turned to the Bible hoping it would show me something of God and his ways. The reading was from the Old Testament book of the prophet Amos. Amos was a rather unpopular prophet, who went around declaring God's anger and impending judgment on the people of his day for their many wrongdoings and wickedness. It wouldn't have been my first choice as a passage of consolation in my loss, but I found it strangely comforting: 'The Lord roars from Zion and thunders from Jerusalem; the pastures of the shepherds dry up, and the top of Carmel withers' (Amos 1:2). Here was evidence in Scripture of God directing hard and difficult events in the lives of people. Thus it *was* God to whom I should turn for possible understanding in this situation. God was the one who was in control of the whole universe. He was the purpose behind all purposes. He was the energy, the creator, the sustainer of all life. He knew everything that had happened and everything that would happen. Mike's death wasn't a freak accident that occurred without God's notice or permission. It didn't negate his sovereignty, his power and design in the world. He knew what had happened, and was going to work out his purposes through it.

Amos compared God to a lion – roaring at his disobedient and wicked creation. I identified with God's anger, the intensity of emotion. God was suddenly much bigger and grander than I had ever imagined. He seemed at once more awful and terrible, and yet at the same time more majestic and wonderful in his patient bearing of the disappointment and grief of the continual disobedience of his people. This passage reminded me of the children's story by C.S. Lewis called *The Lion, the Witch and the Wardrobe*, in which the lion, Aslan, the king of the beasts, is symbolic of Christ:

But as for Aslan himself, the beavers and the children didn't know what to do or say when they saw him. People who have not been in Narnia sometimes think that a thing cannot be good and terrible at the same time. If the children had ever thought so, they were cured of it now. For when they tried to look at Aslan's face they just caught a glimpse of the golden mane and the great, royal, solemn, overwhelming eyes; and then they found they couldn't look at him and went all trembly.[2]

In the dimness of the morning light, I asked, 'Who are you, God?' I realised that although I had been a Christian for many years, in reality I hardly knew him at all.

I dragged myself out of bed and wandered downstairs to the kitchen. My mother was already up, and once again had tended to James. We chatted about how Mike was such a fine man, and yet again said how we could hardly believe that he was gone. The whole of our family would miss him dearly.

My parents-in-law, Ann and Douglas, and Mike's sister, Maggie, and his brother, David, were due to arrive from England that afternoon. We were pleased that they were able to come over for the funeral. We knew that if Mike's death seemed an awful shock to us, that it must seem to them an even greater unreality – having occurred thousands of miles away across the ocean.

Mum and Fiona offered to look after James for me while Dad and I drove to the airport to meet them. I tried to dress neatly and to compose myself. As Dad searched for a parking space, I stood by the doors waiting for them to come through customs.

I looked around at all the people bustling around me. It was so noisy and busy. Everyone was rushing this way and that. I wondered about their situations, and what each family was facing. I realised that I just didn't know what difficulties other people had to face. One young woman, obviously waiting for a passenger from the same plane, glanced at me and struck up a conversation. 'Who are you waiting for?' she asked. 'I'm waiting for my husband. He's been on a business trip.'

I replied, 'My parents-in-law; my husband died a few days ago and they are coming over for his funeral.' She looked exceedingly embarrassed and just said, 'Oh.' Our conversation came to an abrupt halt.

Finally, I spotted Maggie and David coming through the glass doors. I waved to them, and tears welled up in my eyes as I noticed that they looked tired and strained. Maggie and I hugged, and David and I kissed each other on the cheek. My parents-in-law followed and I found myself enveloped in Mike's mother's arms. We held each other in a long embrace, both freely crying over a man we both dearly loved. 'Catherine, we're so, so sorry. You know we love you,' said Ann gently.

When we got back to my parents' home, Ann and Douglas met James for the first time. This was a very poignant moment for them; Mike should have been here to introduce them to his new son.

My parents prepared a light meal for us all, and we spent the evening recounting our experiences and reactions to Mike's death. 'People have been so kind,' said Ann. 'Between family and the church, all our air fares were paid for!' My mother commented in return, 'Friends here have been marvellous too. One church friend of mine has provided several meals for us. Yes, people have been wonderful, but it's been a terrible shock to us all. Mike was very special to us.'

'We considered him one of our own,' Dad agreed.

'Thank you,' Ann said, lifting up the corners of her mouth into a sad smile. 'He was pretty special to us, too.'

We all discussed our initial attempts to try to under-stand Mike's sudden and unexpected death. We saw

God at work, through the help and comfort provided by his people, and we confirmed our belief that God was all-knowing and all-powerful – and so somehow in ultimate control of the situation. But we admitted that we didn't understand why God let it happen.

Douglas said, 'We are not asking "Why?" We leave that to God. Our place is to put our trust in him.' Ann recalled the words in a card that someone had sent to them: 'We don't know why, but we know why we trust God, who knows why.'

Each of us was lost in his or her own thoughts for a while, pondering on these profound statements. I trusted in God too, but I admitted to myself that I also had doubts. 'Lord, I believe; help my unbelief' said one man to Jesus. It was confusing. If I was honest, I did want to know why God had let this happen. I wanted to know how Mike's death fitted into the scheme of things – not in order to rail bitterly against God, but as a means of helping me to come to terms with this loss. I couldn't understand how an all-powerful loving God, which he claimed to be, could allow pain and suffering and death. Yet the reality was that somehow these things are included in his plans and purposes in the world as it is at present. Why didn't God prevent it from happening? I felt that he had protected me in the past – so why hadn't he protected Mike, one of his servants? If he was in control of this world, then there ought to be some explanation for his apparent inaction in this situation. Or was he arbitrary, capricious? Or was he far away and just didn't care? These questions were much too difficult for me to answer. All I could try to hold on to were God's words to Isaiah: 'so are my ways higher than your ways and my thoughts than your thoughts' (Isaiah 55:9b).

I couldn't deny God's love and goodness as it was being demonstrated overwhelmingly in the love and concern expressed by so many family and friends, but it didn't explain why he let Mike die in the first place. I needed to discover the meaning of Mike's death. My faith had always been based on my knowledge and my experience. As a good 'IVCFer', I had done much thinking about my faith and how it related to all aspects of my life and work. My faith wasn't a jump in the dark after my understanding reached its limit, but rather a commitment to God based on my knowledge of the world and of him. If my faith was worthwhile keeping, then it must be rooted in reality. Thus I wrestled with the paradox of a loving God and the existence of pain and injustice in the world he created.

My mother broke suddenly into our individual thoughts: 'Dr Baxter will be coming round shortly, he'll be giving the address at the funeral service tomorrow. He'd like to talk to you about the services.' He arrived shortly after we finished dinner, and warmly greeted Mike's family. They remembered each other from our wedding. Gently and sensitively, he went over the plans for the next day. 'Catherine wants to go to the mortuary to view Mike's body; this is going to be difficult, because of the head injuries he received. Do you want to go along too?' He turned to Douglas and Ann.

'We don't need to see him,' Douglas replied, 'we'd prefer to remember him as he was. But we would like to go with Catherine to the funeral parlour.'

'That's settled then,' said Dr Baxter. 'Now, Douglas, would you like to read the Scriptures or lead prayers at the service tomorrow?'

Douglas amazed me by saying yes. How could a father manage to speak at his son's funeral, I wondered. It suddenly hit me what an extraordinary loss this was for them. It was all out of order – a son shouldn't die before his parents. I felt proud of my parents-in-law that they had such strength of faith. It helped me to see that God was giving them strength, as he was me. I had often felt bad about them being so far away, that Mike was over here in Canada. After all, it was partly because of me that he had stayed here. Perhaps if he had found work in England, this would never have happened. Yet it seemed pointless and useless to keep saying 'if only . . .' It wasn't going to bring Mike back. But it really was hard not to keep wondering if things could have been different. Yet Mike and I really did believe that we were where God wanted us to be; and Mike was certainly doing brilliantly in his work with IVCF. Nevertheless, I felt very grateful to Mike's parents that they didn't in any way blame me for what had happened.

By this time, we were all tired, and my parents-in-law decided to go to bed to rest from their journey and prepare themselves for the funeral service on the following day. Maggie and I followed shortly after – we were sharing a room together. As we got ready for bed, I turned to Maggie and said, 'I'm so glad you could come. It means so much to me to be with you; you understand what it's like. I know how much you loved him – and he, you.' 'He wasn't just my brother,' Maggie said, 'he was my best friend.' We hugged each other tightly, in mutual understanding of the deep hurt and shock of our loss.

I woke early the next morning and turned again to my Scripture notes. I was to read again from the Book of Amos: 'For three sins of Judah, even for four, I will not turn back my wrath' (Amos 2:4). It hit me that there was something inscrutable and uncompromising about God. He hated sin:

'I gave you empty stomachs in every city and lack of bread in every town, yet you have not returned to me,' declares the Lord. 'I also withheld rain from you when the harvest was still three months away. I sent rain on one town, but withheld it from another. One field had rain; another had none and dried up.

People staggered from town to town for water but did not get enough to drink, yet you have not returned to me,' declares the Lord (Amos 4:6–8).

Here was an example in the Bible of God using hardships in the lives of people in order to bring them back to himself. It made me think of the apostle Peter when he remonstrated with Jesus for telling his followers that he was going to be captured by wicked men, suffer and die. Peter denied that God would let such an awful thing happen, but Jesus turned on him with a harsh rebuke and said, 'Get behind me, Satan!' I found myself wondering what kind of God could let his only son, whom he loved, experience such excruciating pain and death. Yet I knew the answer was because he loved us so much, because Jesus' death was a sacrifice on our behalf, which in turn brought new life for us. God was at once more awful and terrible, and yet more compassionate and self-sacrificing, than I had ever before imagined. In my limited human perception I identified with Peter: I cringed from the harshness of pain and death; I wanted to avoid it, to ignore it, to deny its existence. But since it had touched me personally, I could not. Yes, God's ways were vastly different from mine, way beyond my comprehension or imagining.

If I were God, I thought, I would make life nice and easy; I would never allow babies to die of AIDS, children to die of cancer, people to be tortured for their beliefs, thousands to suffer from the ravages of war, many more to die of starvation and sickness in refugee camps. Perhaps until Mike's death I had life too easy; I had never really had to face up to the reality of life's hardships. Suddenly, some lines of C. S. Lewis came to me. I think they go something like this: 'God whispers to us in our pleasures, speaks to us in our conscience, but shouts in our pain: it is his megaphone to rouse a deaf world.'[3]

'OK, Lord,' I prayed. 'You've got my attention. I see that you sometimes use hard situations to bring people back to yourself. But how does this apply to me? You know that I already trusted you. I know you are not punishing me for my past sins; you forgave me for them long ago. I have experienced so much of your grace and mercy – you know how much I love you. Yet I will turn to you. I need you. And I know that Mike's death wasn't to punish him – he wasn't perfect, but he was certainly in right relationship with you. Was it to bring other people to yourself? I do hope that this will bring some people closer to you, but I can't say that if someone comes to Jesus through this, that it would be "worth it". I can't believe that that is the reason *why* it happened. Mike was a natural evangelist. He was so easy-going and open about his faith that you could have continued to use him in that way. Yet, I do know that you can bring good out of bad, life out of death, so I do pray that you will bring people to yourself through this.'

Suddenly I heard Maggie stir; it was time to get up. I closed my Bible, not fully understanding what God was doing, but comforted to know that he was in control and with us. Maggie and I prayed that he would give us strength and composure for the day.

5

Rituals and Reflections

'Simon Peter answered him, "Lord, to whom shall
we go? You have the words of eternal life"'
(John 6:68).

The funeral was to be held in the afternoon, but I decided
that before this I would go to the mortuary to see Mike's
body. I wanted to kiss him goodbye; he had forgotten
to kiss me before he left on that tragic morning, and
it still hurt. Even though I knew he could no longer
respond to me, I needed to say goodbye to him before
he was buried.

Both my parents and Mike's family came with me
to the mortuary. We were a solemn group on that
bleak wintery morning. We pushed open the doors
of the funeral parlour and stepped on to the thickly
carpeted foyer. Everything was hushed and subdued.
Like a very grand hotel, there were settees strategically
placed for our comfort, and a few potted plants standing
in corners. Glass-topped coffee and side tables gleamed,
with ornaments and vases decorating their tops.

Dr Baxter and Don Posterski entered the foyer from
within the building and walked out to greet us. This was
unexpected – what were they doing here? What did this
mean? Don invited the others to come and sit down on
the cushioned settees and Dr Baxter asked me to follow

him. He led me around the corner to another beautifully furnished room. It looked like an executive's office with a huge dark mahogany desk and rich tan leather chairs polished to a shine. I was too taut and nervous to sit down, so I leaned slightly on the desk for support.

I looked at Dr Baxter enquiringly. 'What's going on? I didn't know you would be here. Is something wrong? Couldn't they fix Mike up like they said they would – enough for me to see him?'

'No, Catherine, they couldn't. I'm so sorry,' he said gravely. I felt completely crushed. I had been waiting for five days to see him, and now they were saying it was impossible. My pent-up emotion burst out, and I sobbed and sobbed on Dr Baxter's broad shoulders.

'But I need to see him,' I sobbed. 'To know that they didn't make a mistake – to say goodbye. We never had a chance to say goodbye.' I broke down again.

'I know. Catherine, we don't recommend it. Don and I went to see him and it just isn't Mike – not as we remembered him.' Dr Baxter tried to comfort me, but part of me just wanted to rebel at this protection. Slowly, I composed myself. I did understand their concern. I didn't want to remember Mike bruised and broken; I wanted to remember him as he was. Reluctantly, I walked back to the others; I felt completely helpless and utterly defeated.

Then my mother put forward a suggestion. 'Would you like to see only the lower half of his body and to remove his wedding ring?'

I thought about this for a moment. 'Yes, I think I would.' Mum checked out her suggestion with the mortician, who agreed to cover up Mike's face with a sheet.

'I would like to go on my own, if I may,' I requested Mike's parents, Maggie and David stayed seated on the settees in the foyer. My parents acknowledged my wish

or privacy, but they, along with Dr Baxter, accompanied
me up the stairs. We turned right at the top of the stairs
and saw an open door to an empty room in which lay an
open coffin lying on the floor, perpendicular to the door.
Dr Baxter held out his arm to hold my parents back, and
the three of them let me go in alone.

Slowly, I walked forward and looked down at the body
in the coffin lying motionless, its top half covered by a
white sheet. Mike was dressed in his one dark suit, his
best shirt and a red tie. His hands were resting still by
his sides. There was no mistake; it was Mike. 'Oh, my
beloved,' I said quietly. I raised his hands and held them
in mine. I gazed at his sensitive hands: hands that used
to comfortably hold mine on evening walks; hands that
had spent many hours of careful writing, when he did
his studies; hands that caught rugby balls and made
snowballs. Yet they were hands that were now bruised
and cold. Carefully I removed his wedding ring from
his ring finger on his left hand. It was not easy; rigor
mortis had set in and his finger was slightly bent. For a
moment, I wanted to throw the sheet back to see his face
and hug him, but I knew that the others were standing
at the door behind me. I slipped the ring over my thumb
and rose to go.

Wordlessly, the others followed me back down the
stairs. At the bottom, a lady approached me to offer
me a cup of coffee. I politely declined – I couldn't
bear the thought of social chit-chat at that moment. I
didn't want to be rude, but it felt like an intrusion. I
So I turned to the others and asked, 'Could we go
home now, and have coffee there?' Slowly, I walked
out of the building and over to the car. I needed to
be alone with my own thoughts. Once more, the same
old questions swirled around in my head. How could
God allow such damage to a person? Was God calmly
looking down from his universal station tower, casually

acknowledging that another person had died? Was God some kind of cosmic sadist knocking down his creatures one by one: this one to cancer, that one to a heart attack, another in a car accident? Was the world merely a giant chess game in which he captured men like pawns? Was God untouched by a skull crushed beyond recognition? How could a loving God do such a thing? Then, in the midst of my pain, I remembered Someone else marred beyond recognition, crucified on a cross. I felt God's hurt and anger along with mine. He not only sympathised; he grieved with me. Yes, if he was in ultimate control of the world he had *allowed* it to happen, but he didn't *cause* it to happen. Not everything that happens is 'his will'. It was too simplistic to attribute all events directly to him. After all, death wasn't part of his original intention for human beings.

God created human beings as persons like himself, loving and good, to live in fellowship with himself. No, I couldn't blame God for Mike's death. It wasn't God's fault that death entered the world. It was Satan who introduced evil and hatred into the world, and human beings who were this wicked master's willing slaves.

In the biblical story of the beginning of human existence, the first man and woman, Adam and Eve, destroyed the fellowship they had with their Creator by defying the one restriction that he had given them. They weren't content to live in innocence, but wanted knowledge of good and evil. They were deceived by Satan into thinking that this knowledge would make them become like God. But their disobedience did just the opposite – they were now tarnished by evil and wickedness. Satan also deceived them into thinking that God wouldn't really punish them as he had said he would. But God was true to his word, and their deliberate disobedience produced dire consequences. As they had failed to live as he had intended them to live, to be what he had created them to be, he set a limit to their existence.

But if God subjects people to death and decay, is he cruel? No. In him is no darkness; no evil motives or desire for revenge muddy his intention. He is holy and good; his judgments are just. It is human beings, by their wickedness, who have multiplied the pain and suffering and death in this world. Assault and murder, war and oppression are crimes committed by people, not God. Sickness, pain and death are the result of sin – the sin of the author of sin, the evil one – and the sin of human beings. God is the author of life and continues to sustain all life and goodness; death and destruction are a direct negation of his work of creation.

How deeply disappointed God must be in humanity, the pinnacle of his creation. Yet he didn't just wipe them off the face of the Earth; death wasn't God's final answer to human beings' refusal to be what they were meant to be. He had a plan to restore people to himself.

He subjected the world also to decay and death. The trials and tribulations people would face from then on revealed their need of him and so would draw them back to himself. In the New Testament Book of Romans, chapter 1, St Paul describes how God 'gave men over to their sin' – that is, let them continue in their sin so they could observe and experience the consequences of their sin and in order to recognise their wickedness, see their need of God, and turn back to follow him.

Does that mean that for God the end justifies the means? Is God still good if he uses pain and suffering as a means of drawing people back to himself? This assumption neglects to acknowledge the influence of Satan and the element of human folly and failure. It is human beings who have caused the decay and destruction in the first place – God is just using all things, even our weakness and wickedness, to restore his just and loving rule.

God still saw some good in his creation, and refused to restrict people's freedom of choice because of their rebellion. Humans still retained their ability to choose to follow him and his goodness, or to reject his love and goodness and choose their own way in selfishness and wickedness. He could have changed humans into automatons, robots, who would automatically do his bidding. But God would not remove the original worth and dignity of persons. God maintained human beings' likeness to himself in this way, even though this image had now become distorted. God still offers the opportunity for his people to turn back to him, but people choose evil over and over again. I was no different; I am part of wicked humanity and continue to rebel against my Creator.

Although I did nothing to cause Mike's death, I have no right to complain that I do not deserve this loss. I can't ask 'Why do bad things happen to good people?' like Rabbi Kushner does in his book of a similar title, in which he struggles to understand the tragic illness and early death of his son.[1] I don't claim to be good, but it is a fact of life that people do not always get what they deserve. Many times the wicked do go unpunished, and even prosper, while those who try to be good and kind are often poor and victimised. Life on earth *isn't* fair; God never said that it would be. Sometimes we have to wait until the next life before wrongs are righted and justice is realised.

In one sense, as well as being a punishment, death was a form of mercy. By subjecting all humankind and the world to decay and death, God prevented the eternal existence of evil and wickedness, which has now permeated the world. Death of the perpetrators of wickedness produces the possibility of an ultimate cessation of the selfishness and strife now an inevitable and integral part of life on this earth.

Yet death wasn't God's last word in his dealings with

humankind. God did more than just punish; he planned himself to enable us to return to him. He promised to send someone to save people from their punishment and ultimately to defeat death.

That someone was Jesus. In the Bible it says that Jesus revealed the mystery of God, that in him God dwelt in bodily form. In Jesus, God came and took the punishment in our place.

I started to think again about Jesus' life. He never sinned; he did not fight evil with evil. He was taken by wicked men and was tortured and crucified. Jesus willingly took in all the evil of man, but instead of fighting back, he accepted the pain. He could have fended off his adversaries at any time by sword or angel, but instead he offered himself as a sacrifice for us. Ever since then, as a result of his death, others have life. No, God does not sin. In fact, quite the opposite. He fights evil with good, hate with love.

So how does all this fit in with Mike's fatal accident? No one had evil intent. God wasn't punishing those involved for some specific sin they had committed. Most were his people, accepted because of their faith in Jesus, and continually admitting their sins and turning away from them. It was an accident: bad weather conditions; human physical limitations; bad visibility from a hill; a lorry coming at the exact instant that the minibus went out of control and skidded on to the oncoming lane.

I began to see that there is a common suffering just as there is common grace. We are all under the curse of death and decay since the fall of man. We know that 'the whole creation has been groaning as in the pains of childbirth right up to the present time' (Romans 8:22). One doesn't have to look far to see pain and suffering of all sorts throughout the world. But that is not the end of the story: 'Neither death nor life . . . nor anything else in all creation, will be able to separate us from the love of

God' (Romans 8:38–9). God is working to bring creation back under his just and loving rule, and will one day make all things new. For a while, the devil has his sway, but some day God will crush Satan and punish evil-doers (Genesis 3:15). His justice and peace will reign; there will be no more sorrow or tears or mourning.

The knowledge that God identified with me in my grief, and was working things for good, gave me the strength and courage to get through Mike's funeral. My mother had recently bought me a straight ankle-length cream-coloured skirt and matching cardigan. It was smart, yet not dark and dreary. I knew it wasn't the usual outfit of a widow, yet somehow it seemed appropriate. I had no desire to wear black; this was my way of affirming that I believed that Mike was alive and with God.

Friends stayed at my parents' home to take care of James and to look after my uncle. The rest of us bundled into cars to participate in this very important ritual; to acknowledge publicly our personal loss, but also to affirm our trust in God, who cares for us.

The sky was grey and heavy; the wind was chill and brisk. The coldness matched my heart, which was lonely and sad, yet just as our winter coats kept us from feeling the full harshness of the winter, God's presence wrapped around me in protection. It didn't shield me from reality, but God held me firmly in his care.

The church car park was overflowing, but we found a parking place reserved for us. The family walked in to the church by the side door to go into the church lounge where the last-minute plans were confirmed. My brothers, Mike's brother and the IVCF student president, Jim, were all to be pallbearers.

We entered the church sanctuary by the left-hand door near the front. The first couple of rows of pews had been reserved for us. I briefly glanced around as we sat down, and was amazed to see so many people. Even the balcony

was full to bursting, and people were still pouring in.
They had to file into the choir loft as well, so they
had to sit facing us. I think some of these people felt
embarrassed by this seating arrangement, but I didn't
mind. At that moment I was composed; I focused my
thoughts on the people to help me hold back the tears.
What an enormous number of people! There were friends
I hadn't seen for years – some all the way from Ottawa,
hundreds of miles away.

There was a hush as the organist started to play. It
was so heartening to see how widely loved and respected
Mike was, and I felt proud to have been his wife – even
if it was for such a short time. I had no regrets about my
time with him at all. The sharp pain of his loss could not
remove the warmth of the love and companionship that
we had shared.

The minister of this church was himself in hospital,
fighting cancer, so Dr Baxter led the service. Don
Posterski spoke about Mike and his work with IVCF,
and acknowledged how much he would be missed. He
said out loud what many of us were thinking: that the loss
of Mike was so hard to take because he was really just
starting out. Yet Don encouraged us to face the reality of
his death with the faith that it somehow fitted into God's
greater plan in the world.

Mike's father, Douglas, read the lesson: '"Someone
may ask, 'How are the dead raised?' . . . What you sow
does not come to life unless it dies . . ." [1 Corinthians
15:35–6]. What shall we say in response to this? If
God is for us, who can be against us? . . . neither
life, nor death . . . nor anything else in all creation
will be able to separate us – or Michael – from the
love of God that is in Christ Jesus our Lord' (Romans
8). Douglas's strong voice, and the personal inclusion of
Mike in the reading, spoke volumes of God's strength
and provision.

Then John Bowen prayed a prayer:

Heavenly Father, where were your love and power when we needed them? . . . Thank you that we can bring to you our confusion and our doubts, our anger and pain to you and you will still welcome us . . . Jesus has shown us that you are a God who weeps over death, are angry at evil. We know that you lost your only son through a violent death. As we mourn, may we know your presence is very real, weeping and feeling the pain as we do.

His prayer echoed my thoughts and feelings completely. John Bowen wasn't pretending that this loss didn't hurt, but he showed that the reality of God was even deeper. I felt encouraged and assured of God's love and presence.

We sang the hymn that Mike and I had sung at our wedding:

. . . bear patiently the cross of grief or pain leave to thy God to order and provide in every change he faithful will remain

. . . when dearest friends depart and all is darkened in the vale of tears then shalt thou better know his love, his heart who comes to soothe your sorrows and fears

. . . the hour hastening on . . . when disappointment, grief and fear are gone sorrow forgot, love's purest joys restored.

(We Rest on Thee)

Dr Baxter preached on the Christian hope of eternal life with God, and affirmed our belief that Mike had gone home to be with his heavenly Father. He acknowledged that Mike had departed from us, but just like the Irish folk of his youth, who boarded ships to sail for the new country of North America, Mike had a destination ahead, a new home to go to, one that was sure and wonderful, a home with his Lord.

The service concluded with one of Mike's favourite hymns, 'The day thou gavest, Lord, has ended . . .' Tears streamed down my face, but I didn't care; I wasn't ashamed of my grief.

I felt deeply inspired and comforted. The service was magnificent. It acknowledged the pain and hurt of Mike's sudden and untimely death, yet also declared the hope of God in our midst. Far from an ordeal to be endured, I found the funeral a means of grace. I had refused to take a tranquilliser to dull my senses, but instead allowed the service to speak to me and concentrated hard throughout. I felt that the beginnings of healing had taken place deep within my soul. The tight knot of doubt and sorrow in the pit of my stomach loosened, and I was given courage and hope to press on.

At the end of the service, the pallbearers carried the coffin down the aisle out of the church; the immediate family followed, starting with the front row of pews. Maggie and I held hands as we walked down the aisle. It seemed peculiarly like a wedding procession, and I thought what a contrast to Mike's and my joyful march out of the church at our wedding only two and a half years before. On that day, Mike and I were smiling with joy and happiness as we had just become husband and wife; now we had been torn apart and I had to carry on without him. As we reached the door of the church, a funeral attendant placed a single rose in my hand. I didn't know what it was for, but I clasped it in my hand as we braved the swirling snow once again to drive to the burial site.

There then followed some misunderstanding and confusion, resulting in neither the ministers nor the pallbearers following us to the cemetery. My father drove me,

Mike's parents and sister Maggie, and my mother followed in a second car with Mike's brother, David. The funeral director was as confused as we were, so we waited for a while for the others to arrive. Without the pallbearers, it meant that there was no one to carry the coffin to its burial site.

In the end, Mike's father, brother and my father had to lift the coffin out from the hearse, and place it on wooden planks covering a recently dug hole. We stumbled along the snowy ground as we followed them to the grave-side where his remains were to be placed. As Mike's immediate family and my parents and I stood surrounding the coffin, there was an uncomfortable silence. No one was sure what to say. Dr Baxter had said the words of committal at the end of the funeral, 'Dust to dust, ashes to ashes . . .', announcing that the family was going to have a private burial. It suddenly occurred to me what I was to do with the rose, which was still prickling my palm. I placed it on the coffin and whispered, 'Goodbye, my love.'

As we turned to go back to the cars, a sense of unreality took over. We looked back to see Mike's coffin clearly visible against the flat ground, since all the headstones were laid flat at ground level. Only the occasional winter shrub broke the white coldness of the scene. Maggie and I looked at each other in mutual bewilderment. It seemed such a bizarre situation. I thought of Mike dressed for eternity in trousers taped up with masking tape, and had to stifle a nervous giggle. I could almost hear him say, 'Catherine, you could at least have sewn up my trouser leg.' None of it seemed real. There was Mike's body lying cold in the ground when he was still so alive in our memories. We affirmed that his soul was surely alive with God. We found ourselves wondering what Mike thought about it all – was he watching this strange scene?

Back at the church, the people who had attended the funeral were waiting for our return. They were anxious to greet us and to express their condolences. We headed towards the lounge where refreshments were being served, but so many people stopped us on the way that it was impossible to get that far.

It was incredible to see so many friends from our different places of residence, different activities and associations. Each one had a specific memory of Mike to share. I was touched by their care and mutual love for him. There were over thirty people from Ottawa where we used to live – they had travelled over 300 miles to get to Toronto. Some were friends from Carleton University; some were from our church. There were students, professors, ministers, dear friends and family. Others were from Hamilton; students and supporters from ICVF; neighbours and friends, church associates and work colleagues. Somebody estimated that there were about 700 people at the funeral.

It was nearly two hours later before I made it to the fellowship room where the rest of the family were standing together. The warmth of so many people's love and care gave me comfort and consolation. I wasn't alone; there were many people who shared my loss and who were with me. They gave me confidence. I turned to Mike's family and announced to them that I would still like to go over to England for Maggie's wedding in May. Mike and I had already contacted a travel agent to obtain flight bookings for the trip.

Maggie and I embraced. We would try hard to face the future without Mike.

A week after Mike's death, my mother, Mike's parents and I went to the Sunnybrook Hospital to visit the two girls who had received spinal cord injuries in the accident. Caroline's parents were there and were feeling encouraged; although she was still in much pain and required much more physiotherapy, the indicators were that she would walk again. In Geraldine's case, the news was not nearly so positive. As she still had no recovery of sensation, it looked as if her spinal cord had been so severely damaged that she would probably be paralysed for life.

Geraldine and I shed tears together at the harshness of her prognosis and the loss of Mike, and the waste of young life generally. Yet she was grateful to be alive, and I could see she would fight to regain as much mobility as possible. In spite of her daunting disability, she was so delightful and loving that I believed that she would somehow be all right.

As we drove home through the dark grey clouds of winter rain, I felt sad and forlorn. Life now seemed so grey and dreary. The ultimate harshness of reality impressed itself upon me. There seemed to be no softening of the blow, no cushioning of the pain. Life wasn't easy, and I wondered for the umpteenth time, 'Why, Lord? Why didn't you protect them?' There was no response forthcoming, yet I knew I couldn't deny God's existence.

On the Sunday following the funeral, I woke up in a deep depression. My throat was sore and my chest ached. I remembered some of Mike's little ways, and once more I wept. The sorrow was so heavy that it felt as if it was weighing me down and enveloping me like a thick fog, obscuring all thought. I felt completely listless, but I knew we had to pack up and drive to Hamilton for the memorial service. I had to keep blinking back tears so I could see where I was going as I drove my parents-in-law to my home. I felt so tired, numb and weary.

It was so strange returning to the house in Hamilton without Mike. It wasn't large or grand, merely a modest semi-detached home. Yet it was comfortable, and more than adequate for our needs. We had been so pleased to find it just before James was born.

I was amazed to find it tidy – not the tip that we had left it in when we set off for that last weekend at the cottage. Flowers adorned the coffee table. I went upstairs to change, and noticed that Mike's jumpers had been tidied away. I realised that Julie and her husband, Dave, must have done all this for me. I was so grateful for their thoughtfulness, yet the lack of clutter only seemed to accentuate the absence of Mike.

The memorial service was to be held at two o'clock in the afternoon. Unlike the day of the funeral, I did not feel strong and composed; I just felt tired and weak. I had no desire to meet people, and it took a tremendous effort to enter the chapel in front of the large crowd who were filling every available seat.

The service was different in design and focus from the funeral itself. Several people shared various memories of Mike, often recalling jokes and anecdotes concerning him. But my sense of humour was severely lacking, and I found it very hard to concentrate. However, there was a violin duet that was soothing. John Bowen gave the address, again giving words of encouragement. He quoted from John: 'unless a grain of wheat falls to the ground and dies, it remains only a single seed. But if it dies, it produces many seeds' (John 12:24). He dared to address the difficulty of Mike's untimely death. It seemed to be so senseless, so useless, such a waste. Yet John Bowen gave us hope in the mysterious biblical principle of resurrection that God is able to bring life out of death. It was encouraging to hear others believe that God would bring good out of this apparent tragedy.

Mike's parents again participated, sharing some childhood memories of Mike. Don Posterski affirmed that God was already at work, touching people's lives. He mentioned how one of the girls who was injured in the accident, Kathy, was seriously reflecting on her need for God and considering becoming a Christian. He urged us to face the reality of Mike's death by stating that he would no longer be at their directors' meetings. He said that they would have an empty chair representing Mike at their next meeting, but at subsequent meetings that they would not, because 'life invites us to go on'.

For my part, though, I wasn't feeling ready to 'go on'. My world had stopped, and I felt disoriented and depressed. It was an effort to make it through each day, and a lot of the time I couldn't care less what was happening in the rest of the world.

The time immediately after the memorial service was reminiscent of the funeral, with so many people coming up to us to share in our loss. Renate's parents had graciously and courageously come to the service, having just buried their daughter the previous day. Students and parents of the injured, IVCF supporters, friends and acquaintances, all identified with us in our grief. A couple whom Mike and I had briefly got to know through our antenatal classes handed me a photo of all the babies of our class lined up on a settee with the new parents standing and kneeling around them. It was taken less than a fortnight before Mike had died.

It was after five o'clock in the evening when people finally started drifting off, and we bundled into our coats to return home. My parents came back with us to the house. Friends and family provided food, and James's babysitter, Colleen, prepared a delicious buffet supper for us. I hadn't even thought as far ahead as tea. We sat around in my sitting-room, and again I was overwhelmed by the love and care shown by family and friends.

My parents then returned to Toronto, with promises that they would be back to visit me in a few weeks. Mike's parents stayed with some other friends in Hamilton, but Maggie and David stayed with James and me. That night, for the first time since the accident, I slept in the bed that Mike and I had once shared, and yet again the painful memories flooded back. When I awoke, my pillow was damp with tears and my eyes puffy.

But I knew I had to battle on. I had James to look after, and there were financial matters to be attended to. Cards and condolences were still pouring in, and Mike's family were a big help in a variety of ways. Everything seemed to take so long to sort out. I was deeply grateful to the couple, IVCF supporters, who were putting up Mike's parents. They invited David, Maggie and me over for a meal in the evening, which relieved me of the responsibility of thinking about cooking, and also provided some relaxing company.

Everyone was so supportive and caring. The verse 'blessed are those who mourn' (Matthew 5:4), although perhaps being taken out of context, seemed to be true for me. Although no one could take away my grief, everyone's care brought a measure of healing and consolation. It helped me to share the loss with others, to have company in my distress.

The overwhelming response of friends and acquaintances in cards and letters was also a comfort. However, some cards were not so helpful. One person sent a card with Philippians 4:4, 'Rejoice in the Lord always. I will say it again: Rejoice!' Rejoice? Sorry, I thought, I'm really not in the mood. Didn't it also say in the Bible: weep with those who weep? I thought the person concerned could have picked a more suitable verse under the circumstances. I didn't feel that God wanted us to deny reality and pretend everything was wonderful, or make out that we didn't feel the pain of the loss because we were Christians.

Another card said: 'In God are all the answers to our questions'. Really? He certainly wasn't explaining everything to me right then! Several other people were trying to give answers to the 'why?' question. Some people preached at me, telling me to trust in God and be strong. Others recounted their own losses and claimed that they knew just how I felt. Did they, though? I remembered from my first-year social-work training how 'self-disclosure' ought to be used selectively, not 'overshadowing the client's situation' – and now I knew why!

Another person said, 'Oh, but you'll meet again in heaven.' Yes, I believed that this was true, but knowing the history of longevity in my family, that might not be for another sixty-odd years! This certainly wasn't a tremendous comfort to me at present. It was not that these comments were unchristian, it was just that their timing seemed inappropriate. I wasn't ready to jump to 'victory' yet – I still needed to accept the reality of Mike's death and absorb its impact on my life, step by slow step. I knew from my professional training that grief is a very long-term process, a perilous hike through a deep valley, and as yet I had barely even begun this journey of recovery and readjustment.

One couple, whom I did not even know, told me the story of how their daughter had died many years previously. They said that they had finally come to terms with her death when they accepted that God needed her more than they did. Was I supposed to apply that to my situation? Was I supposed to accept that God really needed Mike more than I did at this time? We had only been married for two and a half years, and we had a two-month-old son. Surely a son really needs his father?

Despite some of the less helpful comments, I knew that people really meant well, and I did appreciate their care and attempts to console me in my loss.

What helped me most was to have people willing just to spend time with me, so that I didn't feel so alone in my grief; and to prevent me from becoming too self-absorbed – or feeling too sorry for myself. I knew depression was never far away, and I didn't have the energy and motivation to attend to all the responsibilities of running a home and responding to the large number of carers and supporters. It meant a lot to me to have help in sorting out the many practical details.

In *The Wounded Healer* by Henri Nouwen,[2] there is a story of a student pastor who is called to minister to a lonely and disheartened man facing serious surgery. The man was rather cynical, and apparently didn't believe in God; he felt discouraged and hopeless. The student pastor struggled to persuade the man to think about God, but the man died during surgery. When Henri Nouwen discussed this case with other theological students, he found that they – like the curate – wanted to challenge the man's incorrect beliefs, but Nouwen suggested an entirely different approach. Instead of arguing points of doctrine with the man, he suggested simply offering to wait for the man – to tell him that he would be there for him after his operation, to relate to him as a person, and give him a reason to live. In a similar way, I felt that my family and friends were 'waiting' with me, and their presence assured me of God's continuing presence. They gave love instead of trying to provide answers, and as Eddie Askew has said, 'Logic loses to love'.[3]

6

Early Days

'So do not throw away your confidence; it will be richly rewarded. You need to persevere so that when you have done the will of God, you will receive what he has promised' (Hebrews 10:35–6).

The formal ceremonies of the funeral, burial and memorial services provided a useful public opportunity for friends and family to express their love and sympathy at my loss. These public expressions of grief were now over, but my private grief was still in its initial stages. As yet, I did not feel able simply to carry on with life – as if nothing had happened. My life had been turned upside down; the person who had meant more to me than anyone else in the world was now gone. The one person who had brought me so much happiness and fulfilment in my life was no longer here with me. I needed time to rebuild my life, and re-establish my self-identity.

Yet I couldn't stop life; I needed to keep going. There were numerous practical details to attend to and business affairs to put in order now that Mike had gone. There were loose ends regarding his work that had to be tied up. I had to cancel future engagements he had booked. Funeral expenses had to be paid for, the wording on the headstone chosen. Hundreds of cards and letters still needed my response – not to mention all my responsibilities as a new mother. Feeding, changing and playing with a baby, washing endless nappies. Sometimes all this seemed overwhelming and impossible, particularly when I was feeling so sad and depressed. Emotionally I was drained, and mentally I was preoccupied with my loss. Grieving seemed to take so much emotional energy that I had little left over for anything else.

Words that Elizabeth Elliott had found helpful after her first and second husbands died, 'Do thou the next thing', were an encouragement to me. I couldn't look too far ahead – it really was too daunting – but perhaps I could just face the next task, and then the next, one step at a time. It did seem helpful to try to keep going in this way, so by an act of determination I pressed on.

In one way, James was a big help. A baby's cry is insistent and a baby's needs are persistent. Caring for him helped to keep me going. As I looked after him, I was taken out of myself a little, which kept me from becoming excessively self-preoccupied with my grief and misery. It was hard to focus entirely on my own concerns when I had a beautiful, happy, healthy – and demanding – baby to look after.

The legal and financial matters were more difficult. I knew very little about them, and to be honest I wasn't interested in learning! It was a big help to have the assistance of family members as I tackled these new pressures.

On the Monday morning following the memorial service, Mike's father accompanied me to the bank to help me sort out my finances. I needed to determine whether I could pay bills on our current account; Mike and I had a joint account, so I hoped that I could simply transfer it into my name. The teller wasn't sure of the bank's policy concerning this, so she called the bank manager over.

The bank manager seemed very young and inexperienced. Perhaps to compensate for his youth, his manner was very official and cool. Initially he insisted on following bank policy, requiring that an account must be frozen until the deceased person's estate was settled. I had to explain that Mike didn't have any money, so there was no estate. Finally he relented, and allowed me to pay my bills and the mortgage, and permitted me to open a new account in my name into which cheques could be paid until the estate was cleared. IVCF had already set up the benevolent fund for James and me; and because Mike was working at the time, I was able to claim Workman's Compensation Insurance benefits. These cheques were very helpful in paying my bills, but they were all made out to Mike's estate, so the bank refused to let me pay them in. It was all a very frustrating business, and it took quite a bit of negotiation and discussion before I was finally allowed to pay the cheques into my account. I felt vulnerable and inadequate in dealing with the financial and legal details; this was something that Mike had looked after. Now I was being forced to learn about such things, and required to make decisions I did not feel qualified to make.

Our car insurance was something else that needed sorting out. It needed to be transferred into my name along with the ownership of our car. The insurance company personnel on the other end of the telephone seemed completely indifferent and insensitive to my situation. They transferred me back and forth from one department to another until they finally found someone who could respond to my request. 'My husband died in an accident ten days ago,' I said. But before I could explain further, she interrupted me with, 'Name?' 'Michael Hare,' I began. 'Yes, we have it here – I'll delete it.' With a simple press of the computer button she deleted his name. There seemed no acknowledgment that this was a person we were discussing; her manner was so factual and impersonal. I had to catch her quickly before she rang off, to explain that I didn't in fact telephone in order to have

Mike's name deleted, but to state that the car insurance should now have the name of only one primary driver.

Business matters seemed so complicated and involved. I had little interest in these matters, but now I had to make the effort and to attempt to understand. And it certainly didn't help that the people in these firms seemed to be so lacking in compassion and understanding. This was another harsh reality of life that I was going to have to face.

It also took a great effort to socialise, yet I found it helpful to keep busy and to be involved. I feared that if I cut myself off from people, it would become even more difficult to re-enter social life at a later date, so I vowed, where at all possible, to keep any engagements or involvements that I had made before Mike had died.

Thus when the friends with whom my parents-in-law were staying mentioned the IVCF student meeting the following night, I decided to go. The students were still stunned by the accident in which their staff worker and a fellow student had been killed, and in which some of their friends were seriously injured and disabled. Their faith had been challenged too, and it seemed appropriate to identify with them in their shock and grief. Mike's parents were also concerned for the students, and thought they would like to go too. David and Maggie decided to go as well. In the end, I said, 'Why don't we all go? And I'll take James too. The students would like that – not many of them have even seen him yet.'

The whole business of meeting people after Mike's death felt peculiar. Many people seemed awkward and uncomfortable with me. Sometimes they would avoid me, not knowing what to say. At other times they would stumble around in the conversation – I could tell they wanted to say something, but didn't know how to raise the topic of his death in a delicate way. I supposed that people were uncertain how I would react, and didn't want to upset me even more. It was understandable – and of course different people react in different ways, so they wouldn't automatically know how I felt. What I wanted was to be related to as myself – I was still *me*. Personally, I found it easier to talk about Mike, rather than to avoid any mention of him as if he never existed.

A verse in a book of poetry by a widow, given to me by another young widow, captured my sentiments exactly:

Words

'Words are inadequate.'
How often have I heard that phrase,
Read that phrase,
In the last three months?
How many times have I said it myself?
It's a cop-out.
It justifies saying nothing,
When actually we need to say,
Desperately need to say something.
What's inadequate about
'I'm sorry' or
'I love you' or
'I care'?
What's inadequate about
'You're daily in my prayer'?[1]

It was initially easier for me to spend time with those who knew Mike and shared my loss; and talking about the accident and his death helped me to clarify my thoughts and identify my feelings. It also helped me to begin to make sense of the dark cloud of sorrow and grief. Instead of an undifferentiated mass of confusion and uncertainty, overwhelming and impenetrable, putting my emotions and experience into words helped me gain some sense of control in the situation. It enabled me to break down the grief into manageable parts that were more easy to understand, and into smaller steps less difficult to climb.

The students were delighted to see us at their meeting. James was a helpful ice-breaker, providing an opening for conversation, but also a poignant reminder that his father was now gone. The professor who Mike's parents were staying with led the meeting, giving a survey of the Bible, and showing how – throughout history – God has been faithful in helping his followers whenever they faced hardships and trials. We were able to join in solidarity with the students with our shared faith as well as our shared loss, and to encourage one another to stand firm. When Maggie, David and I returned to my home that evening, we all agreed that we were glad that we had made the effort to go to the meeting.

Mike's family were due to return home to England the following day. I asked Maggie and David if there was anything of Mike's that they would like to take back with them. I hadn't yet touched his belongings, but there was no use in leaving them in cupboards and drawers; he obviously no longer needed them. It would mean more to me to give things to people who knew him, and would appreciate them. David was a similar size to Mike, so I urged him to accept some clothes.

Maggie and I started with his cupboard and chest of drawers. Mike's presence was everywhere: his aroma and fragrance, his style, his enjoyment of dressing up, his enjoyment of sport, his manliness. Yet again, I was overcome with grief. 'Oh Mike, I so miss you,' I thought to myself. Clearing his things out seemed such a strange exercise – how was it possible that material could outlive a person? It seemed so unreal, like a dream from which we would waken. But his clothes were real; all his jumpers and jerseys. Many were given to him for Christmas – some hardly worn and others brand new. It was hard to face the fact that he would no longer have cause to wear his favourite jersey – navy blue with white stripes. Never again would he take me for walks in his bright orange anorak with his tweed cap jauntily tipped over his brow.

I was grateful that I was not clearing out Mike's things on my own, for I would have felt utterly depressed and overwhelmed. It was hard enough as it was. Maggie and I talked and shared our feelings. She suddenly admitted that she felt angry – *really* angry. Her admission seemed to give me permission to acknowledge my own anger. Damn it! Why did a person we loved so much, someone so young, so alive and so full of fun, have to die? It was *wrong*. This wasn't the way it was supposed to be.

Once again, I became aware of God's empathy and understanding. I remembered how Jesus wept at the death of his friend, Lazarus. Jesus knew how we were feeling, and identified with our grief. But of course Jesus then raised Lazarus back to life. God has power over death, for we know that Jesus was crucified and then resurrected to a new life beyond the grave. It did comfort me to know that Mike was with God, and that one day God would remove death. For the moment I was experiencing the pain of Mike's loss, but it wouldn't last for ever: some day I would see God's victory and triumph over this tragedy; some day Mike and I would be reunited in glory.

We packed Mike's things into a suitcase for them to take back with them to England. I gave Mike's mother his fountain pen; and to his father I gave his Harris tweed jacket, one of his jumpers, and a couple of classical tapes from his collection. David took many of Mike's clothes, and Maggie took some for her fiancé. I still felt angry, though. Damn! Damn! Damn! I wanted Mike – not his belongings. Then I recalled a time recorded in the Scriptures when Jesus too was angry. He cursed a fig tree for not bearing fruit to satisfy his hunger, and it withered and died. Was this a glimpse of God's anger at the results of evil in the world? I fancied that God was angry at Mike's death too. After all, Mike was being used by God before the accident. He was a faithful follower, and was learning to preach and to teach others about Jesus. He loved his work with the students, and had dreams of becoming an author and a minister. He had already taken some courses in theology at the divinity college at McMaster University, and had so far obtained straight A grades. Yet Satan, through the evil in the world generally, had cut short Mike's life.

My anger eased somewhat the following morning when I read my Bible. My Scripture Union notes now switched readers to the Book of Genesis, where they examined the life of Joseph, who had been sold as a slave by his brothers. It was a powerful story, giving me hope and assurance that Satan would not have the upper hand. God is all-powerful, all-knowing and all-wise. He knows all the circumstances, all the evil in our hearts, all the details of our lives. Just as God knew all about the scheming and treachery of Joseph's brothers, and was able to turn the situation round for good (Joseph became a powerful leader in Egypt who saved his people from famine), he knew all about the accident and would work in people's lives to bring good out of bad.

Joseph's brothers hadn't reckoned on the extent of their father's grief – all his sons and daughters came to comfort him, but he refused to be comforted: '"No," he said, "in mourning will I go down to the grave to my son"' (Genesis 37:35). Similarly, I didn't think that Satan had reckoned on our grief. I wasn't about to let him get away with this tragedy, and I wasn't going to give in to bitterness just because I didn't understand it. I hoped that this loss would help me grow, and I could already see what influence Mike's life and ministry, and his death, was having on others – perhaps for years to come.

The words of Job, another man of God in the Bible who

faced tremendous losses and troubles, became my prayer:
'I know that you can do all things; no plan of yours can be
thwarted.' God then asked Job, 'Who is this that obscures
my counsel without knowledge?' Job responded, 'Surely I
spoke of things I did not understand, things too wonderful
for me to know' (Job 42:1–3). This seemed to be saying
that God didn't mind my anger or my need to try to
understand Mike's death; he understood. Yet he wasn't
about to explain it all to me – and I wouldn't be able to
grasp it if he tried. I began to recognise that my knowledge
would always be incomplete; my perplexity and curiosity
never entirely satisfied. Perhaps part of coming to terms
with grief was recognising the need to learn to live with
unanswered questions.

We packed up Mike's family's things and all bundled
into the car to take them to the Toronto airport. It was a
very emotional parting. We hugged each other and shed
tears of sadness and of joy. 'I'm so sorry for everything.
Thank you for being so wonderful,' I said to Mike's
parents. I told Maggie that I was looking forward to
coming to her wedding in May. To Mike's father I said,
'I would be honoured if you would be able to baptise
James when we come to England.' Douglas was a lay
minister at Holy Trinity Parish Church in Margate, Kent.
Mike's mother assured me of their love: 'You are our
daughter and you always will be, no matter what the
circumstances, and I know that you will always keep
us informed of our precious grandson.' Their care and
understanding meant so much to me. I knew that Ann
was already thinking about the possibility that I could
one day remarry. Realistically, it was a possibility; I was
still only twenty-nine. Maggie and I had talked about
this, and she said that she and David wanted to give
me a chain for my wedding ring so that I could wear
it around my neck. I was still wearing my ring on my
left hand, yet I had to face the fact that I was no longer

married. I had even told Maggie that if I ever remarried, I would like it to be someone who knew Mike, so that we could remember him together and with James. But I left all this in the Lord's hands – if it ever happened, it would certainly be a very long way off in the future.

Instead of going straight back to Hamilton with James, I stayed with my parents in Toronto for the weekend. My sister Fiona was still visiting from Alabama with her three-year-old son, Christopher. She and my mother helped look after James while I went to see lawyers and to continue sorting out my legal and financial affairs. One of the first things I did was to make my will. By now, I realised only too well how mortal we are; and if I died James would need to be provided for.

My friend Anne, who stayed home from the funeral with her fiancé to look after James and my uncle, called in. She was getting married the following Saturday. 'Catherine, how are you?' she asked. 'You are in my thoughts and prayers.'

'I'm taking it a day at a time,' I replied. 'How about you? How are your wedding plans coming along?'

'Fine, nearly ready. Just some last-minute details to sort out. Will you still be able to come?'

'Yes, of course, you know that I want to be there,' I responded.

'I know that you have lots to cope with at the moment. Do you still want to read the lesson? I could always get someone else to do it if you felt it would be a bit much.'

'Anne, I consider it an honour to participate in your wedding – yes, I'd still like to do it. I think my parents can babysit for me.'

'Catherine, I'm so thrilled that you want to be a part of our special day. You're amazing.' Anne gave me a big hug.

The wedding rehearsal was on the Friday evening, and I sat in the pews as I watched them go through the format and order of service. It was a lovely old stone church with high ceiling and colourful stained-glass windows, inspiring awe and quiet. It was also a little damp and chilly, smelling of musty damp stone, so I kept my coat on. They told me where I was to stand as I read the responsive reading. It was a little strange being among people who didn't know that I had lost my husband just a fortnight before. I had removed my wedding ring before coming, and was very conscious of my return to singleness.

After the rehearsal we sat down to a buffet meal in the hall downstairs, and the priest leading the service ended up at the same table as me and the young bridesmaids. The priest was balding and of medium build. Even in his casual clothes of a polo-neck sweater and jacket, he seemed authoritative as he directed everyone to their places. He was a loud, gregarious person, one who seemed used to being the centre of attention. At the table, he tried to make conversation. He turned to the bridesmaids. 'Hello, what are your names?' He then smiled at me. 'Yes, you're reading the lesson, aren't you? Were you one of Anne's flatmates too?' He didn't mean to be unkind, but he sounded so patronising, talking to me as if I was a young girl, still a student. On the outside I may have looked fairly young, but inside I felt much older because of my recent experience of loss. I wanted to say, 'No, I was married – but my husband has just died', but I knew that this would be rather blunt. Besides, it would just have reflected the conversation back to myself and my recent loss, rather than on Anne and her wedding to be held the following day. So instead I responded, 'No, Anne and I were neighbourhood friends from high school days and from the young people's group and girls' group at my church.'

By the next day, I didn't feel so confident about getting up in front of a crowd to speak. Why did I say I would do it? Would I be emotionally strong enough as I listened to the words 'until death us do part'? But I forced myself to get ready and arrived at the church early. I sat in a pew near the front where I would have easy access to the front lectern. It felt lonely sitting on my own; I was so used to sitting with Mike. The time for reading the lesson soon came, and I walked up to the front of the church and looked out over the large congregation. It was scary looking out over the sea of faces, and I gulped, wondering if I could actually do it. The reading was taken from Psalm 103:

Praise the Lord, O my soul . . . The Lord is compassionate and gracious, slow to anger, abounding in love . . . For as high as the heavens are above the earth, so great is his love for those who fear him . . . As for man, his days are like grass . . . the wind blows over it and it is gone . . . But from everlasting to everlasting the Lord's love is with those who fear him . . . Praise the Lord, O my soul.

I just managed to finish the reading, but my voice started to break at the end, and I ran to find my seat before anyone saw my tears. Once in the pew, I leaned forward and buried my head in my hands as the dam of emotion burst. Someone behind me saw me crying, and slipped a hanky over my shoulder. He was awfully kind, but I felt most embarrassed that he'd noticed. I mopped my damp cheeks and blew my nose, trying to regain control. As I looked up, I was relieved to see that no one other than the people behind me had noticed my display of emotion – for as I had been rushing back to my seat, the photographer was walking across to the altar to take a photograph of the couple, and had tripped over a large flowerpot that fell over with a crash! The congregation were distracted, some saying 'Ooh!' and others chuckling at his clumsiness.

Mercifully, the congregation's distraction meant that I was saved from further embarrassment.

The rest of the service was uneventful, but very meaningful, as Anne and Franco publicly proclaimed their commitment to God and to each other. I joined my parents and some of their church friends at the back of the church to walk round to the halls for the reception. As we waited in the queue to go in, the priest whom I had met the previous night approached me. 'You were marvellous,' he said, 'amazing considering . . . I mean, I know about your, er . . . your, about your husband's, er . . .' His voice trailed off. 'His death,' I said. 'Yes. Thank you.' It amazed me that here was a priest who had ministered to people for over twenty-five years, but couldn't quite bring himself to use the word 'death'.

However, I know that it isn't easy talking about death. It isn't a normal topic of conversation in our society; we try to avoid it at all costs. None of us likes to contemplate our own mortality, and we try to put off facing death for as long as possible. But since Mike's death I could no longer ignore its existence; and in order to recognise its reality, I needed to talk about it, to put it into perspective. Pretending it didn't exist wouldn't make it go away; it was part of life in the world as we know it. Surely if we faced it squarely and honestly, it would lose some of its terror? Perhaps it wouldn't catch us so unprepared.

The reception was a happy celebration, and Anne's and Franco's joy in anticipation of their new life together was visibly apparent. I looked around at the couples near me as we ate our dinner, some young like me, some older, having grown-up children of their own who were also married. Here were Anne and Franco just starting out on their married life together, when my life with Mike was already over. Everyone else seemed to be part of a couple, while I was on my own. I had trouble even admitting it to myself at first, but I realised I was jealous.

I liked being married; we both did. It was a partnership – we shared the work and shared the fun, and we were able to grow together spiritually. But now I was no longer half of a couple; I was single again. From this point on, I would have to go to parties, to weddings, to church and to visit friends on my own. I felt the subtle stigma of being single – even within the Church itself. I tried hard not to feel sorry for myself as I drove with my parents back to their home.

My pastor and his wife paid me a surprise visit. As we sat down to a cup of coffee, I recounted my struggle to read the lesson at Anne's wedding. I admitted that it had perhaps been a little rash of me; it was rather soon after Mike's death to be getting up in front of crowds of people. They smiled at my determination and gave me the affirmation I so needed. They encouraged me to press on, and to be honouring to God and to the memory of Mike. I resolved not to give in to my self-pity; I did not want to give Satan 'a foothold'. Ephesians 4:26 says, 'In your anger [or hurt or sadness] do not sin: Do not let the sun go down while you are still angry, and do not give the devil a foothold.' I made the decision not to become bitter, or to turn inwards and become miserable and lonely. I decided to choose life and happiness over death and sadness, and vowed to carry on as best I could.

As I went to sleep that night I prayed to God: 'Thank you, Lord, for enabling me to choose life and to choose you. Purify me through this fire. I have seen people become disillusioned and cynical from such a loss. I pray that I will not. Please help me to trust you.' I knew that it was going to be very hard, and that the worst was far from over. It had still only been a couple of weeks since Mike had died. I knew that I would go on grieving for a long, long time, and that there would be unguarded moments when memories of Mike would overwhelm me and my heart would break yet again. And I knew that there would be days when I felt that I couldn't go on. The wound was still fresh, but I was slowly learning new things about God and his ways, and I trusted that he was with me and would help me through it.

The love and support of family and friends continued to be invaluable as I took my first stumbling steps forward through the valley of grief. Whenever I found myself sinking into despondency, there was usually someone who dropped by and encouraged me. The company of others prevented me from becoming isolated and lonely in my widowhood.

My sister came back to Hamilton with me, along with her three-year-old son, Christopher. She had one more week before she had to return to her home in Alabama. When we arrived at my house, I walked into the kitchen to put on the kettle to make a cup of tea. To my amazement, there was a microwave oven sitting on my work surface! It was even plugged in and ready to use! I stared dumbly in confusion, wondering where this could have come from, wondering what it was doing there. Then I saw a card lying beside it; I opened it. It was a gift from several different couples that we knew. One of the people was Colleen, who had wondered where my microwave was when she had cooked the meal for us after the memorial service. Tears came to my eyes; I was deeply touched by their thoughtfulness and generosity.

Young Christopher had followed me into the kitchen and was watching me quizzically. He couldn't understand why I had started to cry and piped up, 'What's the matter, Aunty Tatherine, don't you like your pwesent?' I looked down at him and smiled. 'Oh yes, yes I do. Sometimes people cry when they're happy as well as when they're sad.'

It was wonderful having Fiona with me. She helped me in lots of practical ways, by assisting with the cooking and cleaning and caring for James. She was also a

sounding-board as I struggled to make sense of my
emotions and reactions. It was nice to have Christopher
as company for James too. Although Christopher was
only three, he was very good with James, showing him
toys and handing him rattles to keep him occupied.

Fiona had obviously explained to Christopher that
Uncle Mike had died, and that they had come to visit
me to comfort me. He was observing what was going
on and trying to comprehend what was happening. His
innocence and simple faith were sometimes light relief.
One day as we were reading some of the cards and
letters I had received, he turned to me with his childish
curiosity and asked, 'Aunty Tatherine, can Uncle Mike
come back now?'

I bent down and gave him a hug. 'No, Christopher.
Uncle Mike can't come back. He has died and is with
God now.' It is hard enough for an adult to grasp the
finality of death, so it wasn't surprising that three-year-old
Christopher was having difficulty. I wondered how James
would understand what had happened as he grew older.

My best friend Julie also came round, and she helped
me sort through the post to send thank-yous to the
hundreds of people who had sent cards and letters of
condolence and the many who had helped in creative
and practical ways. The pile was so big that the task
had seemed too overwhelming earlier, but I knew I
could not put it off any longer. Julie is a natural
organiser, and she wrote dozens of lists to help me
identify what I needed to do and to prioritise tasks.
This was something that I found difficult at the best
of times, but with my loss of energy and motivation it
seemed nigh-on impossible.

I was touched by the depth of feeling and sympathy
expressed in many of the cards and letters. It was a
great encouragement to know that I was not alone in
my loss, that many others were sharing it with me. Many

expressed how much Mike meant to them, and recalled happy memories of him.

One mother of a camper who trained under Mike at the leaders-in-training programme at Ontario Pioneer Camps was particularly creative in her letter. She enclosed a second letter, addressed to James, for when he was old enough to read it on his own. She told him how much people loved his daddy, and how Mike had helped her son in his Christian walk. She showed incredible wisdom and forethought to prepare for the day when James would want to know more about his father.

One letter was a complete surprise; it came all the way from Nova Scotia. It was from Bruce, the fellow who had asked me out on the same day that Mike had asked me to go out with him. Bruce had since been to the same theological college as me, and was now doing further studies in Nova Scotia in order to train to become a minister.

As we sifted through the letters, I was interested to see a pattern emerging. Most cards simply expressed sadness and sympathy at my loss, but many were trying to come to terms with the accident in light of their faith, and expressed their understanding of God's working in the situation. By and large, people's understanding seemed to fall into two main camps.

One group of people was very affirming and encouraging towards me, saying that God must have considered me special to give me the honour and privilege of overcoming such a tragedy. One part of me found this attitude very difficult to deal with, and I wanted to respond with sarcasm, 'Right – but I could do without being so privileged.' However, my pride, I had to admit, quite liked this explanation. It was nice to be thought of as specially chosen to 'suffer for the Kingdom' as many Christians in the past had done. My martyr complex bloomed and I had visions of grandeur! There might be something to this view, but if I was honest I knew that I was actually quite weak, and certainly no more special than anyone else. Moreover, it was a viewpoint that led me to feel quite sorry for myself – to think that I was much more hard-done-by than anyone else.

Thankfully, no one suggested that I was being punished for my sinfulness through Mike's death, or accused me of having some secret, unconfessed sin that had caused such a calamity in my life. But the second group of people seemed to suggest that God's purpose in this situation was to test my faith; they would then urge me to stand firm and be strong. I could see some truth in this. As in the Book of Job, where Satan questioned God about Job's faith and was given permission to test him, I sometimes felt that I was in a spiritual battle in which I had to fight against blaming and accusing God and against giving in to depression, bitterness and despair.

Yet this particular view caused me to question why I needed to have my faith tested in such a painful and dramatic way. Was I so stubborn and rebellious that I needed a major disaster in order to develop stronger faith? The Book of James was quoted to me, 'Consider it pure joy . . . whenever you face trials of many kinds . . . because you know that the testing of your faith develops perseverance' (James 1:2–3). Did it mean I was so lacking in faith and character that I needed an extra-difficult hardship in order to catch up with others? This way of thinking only provoked feelings of guilt and worthlessness. I knew that I already had faith – it may not have been enormous, but it was real and growing. The Book of Job helped me here. It wasn't because Job was wicked that God allowed his suffering – he was actually described as a good man, and known in his community as a God-fearing man. His trials proved to Satan that his faith was not just based on the benefits God had given him, but his love for God himself.

Again I had to try not to get bogged down in all sorts of complicated theological explanations for my situation. The accident did not occur because I had great faith, or because I had little faith. It didn't necessarily have anything to do with me at all. I knew that I was just an ordinary person, with weaknesses in some areas, and strengths in others. I found the writings of Joni Eareckson very helpful as I struggled with this egocentric introspection. In *A Step Further*,[2] she describes how there appears to be a 'gradient' of suffering in the world. The reality is that some people experience many more hardships than others, but it isn't because they are worse people. Pain is not necessarily fairly or equitably distributed in the world. But one day God will reward everyone justly according to his or her response to his/her circumstances, taking into account the nature and severity of his or her trials. Joni herself is a living testimony. She is a lovely woman, not perfect, but certainly not deserving of the permanent paralysis she has from the neck down as a result of a diving accident.

It is so easy to blame the victim, yet the people who wrote to me weren't doing that at all. Instead, it was *me* who often fell into the trap of blaming myself, by analysing the various theories and taking them to their extremes. In the end, I realised this, and said to God: 'You know my heart, you know that I am weak and sinful, and that I liked the pleasure and prestige of being married. You know that I need to develop in the area of self-discipline, and that I can sometimes be selfish and strong-willed. Please forgive me and cleanse me. But I know also that Mike's death is not a direct punishment from you for some personal sin, and so I give this false guilt over to you.'

Because of the tremendous love and help that Fiona gave me, it was really hard to say goodbye when she had to leave to go back to her home in Alabama. After dropping her off at Toronto airport, I returned home on my own for the very first time since Mike's death. As I lifted James out of his car seat, and turned towards the front door, I said, 'Well James, it's just the two of us now, just us two.' But even as I said the words, one question seemed to repeat itself in my head: 'But *will* I be able to cope on my own?'

7

No Longer the Same

'But Jesus told him, "Follow me, and let the dead bury their own dead"' (Matthew 8:22).

Over the following month, I realised that I was gradually experiencing the reality of life without a husband. The rush of support and help that had upheld me in the first few weeks after Mike's death was now slowly receding; cards and letters, initially pouring in by the dozen, now dwindled to a trickle. I knew that soon they would stop altogether. Other people would go back to their families and carry on with their lives. Yet my world as I had known it had totally collapsed. I wanted to carry on, but nothing was the same.

My energy was depleted, and depression hovered over me like a black cloud. My vision could extend only as far ahead as the next day. I felt weak, and incapable of managing on my own. That I would have to take full responsibility for a household and a child on my own now was a very daunting prospect.

I didn't want to become too dependent on others, but how I wished that someone would come and shovel snow from my driveway, that someone would pop over unannounced just to chat, or look after James so that I could get out for a bit. A poem I had once read seemed to sum up what I was feeling:

Don't Say

Don't say,
'If you need anything, call.'
I need all sorts of things,
But I won't call.
I'm not built that way.
You call me.
Tell me:
'I'll pick up [James] today.'
Tell me:
'Bob will be over to mow the lawn.'
Tell me:
'I'll help you clean today.'
But don't say,
'If you need anything, call.'[1]

But thankfully, I wasn't left totally on my own to cope.
My parents often came to visit at weekends, and their
company helped me a great deal on Friday and Saturday
nights when the house seemed particularly quiet. My
mother helped with some household chores, such as
ironing, cooking meals and looking after James. My
father, being an engineer, was helpful in doing odd jobs
around the house.

Also, my brother's wife, Robin, came over for a few
days at a time with her baby, Benjamin, James's cousin
who was six days older than him. It helped to be able
to compare notes on the eating and sleeping patterns
of our babies, and to get suggestions as to how to
cope with any practical parenting problems. Chatty and
easy-going, Robin helped bring me out of myself. I felt
comfortable with her, able to talk about my feelings and
thoughts since Mike's death. As a fellow Christian, she
encouraged my faith; as a fellow mother, she understood
the ups and downs of caring for a small baby. It was also
a great comfort to have another adult to talk to, someone

with whom I could discuss the challenges and problems of early widowhood.

A widow. What a strange word. It often conjures up images of a sad old lady with grey hair and wrinkles, and dressed in black. As a young woman and a new mother with a generally active social, church and work life, I did not fit the stereotype. I was just at the beginning of what would normally be the most productive years of my life. Yet, as I was beginning to discover, my new identity as a widow did change my social and financial status. I knew that at some point I would have to face this painful reality. First, I needed to come to terms with the fact that I was no longer part of a couple; Mike was no longer around to depend on. He wasn't here to plan and prepare our social outings and holidays; I had to do it myself – in fact, I had to do everything myself. Part of me, in my general state of lethargy, sadness and loneliness, wanted to give up, to crawl into a hole somewhere, and hide away. Yet part of me wanted to carry on as before; and so I pressed on. But it wasn't easy; I missed Mike terribly. I couldn't even go to the shops without thinking of him. When I walked down the aisles, I was overwhelmed with grief as I saw a jar of Marmite. Mike was called the 'Marmite man' by some of his students because he was so addicted to it! And as I walked past the Liquorice Allsorts in the sweets aisle, I felt another pang of loss. Mike used to slip the initials 'L.A.' at the bottom of my shopping list, so I would remember to buy him some.

Wherever I went, whatever I did around the house, I would be reminded of Mike. His little office downstairs was so neat and tidy. He had carefully filed all his notes and IVCF correspondence in his filing cabinet. His calendar for the year was still up on the wall, mapping out his future engagements. His computer still sat on his desk. All his Christian resource books, carefully sorted into subject-matter, filled the bookcase. It was so poignant, yet in a funny way it was also a comfort. At times it seemed as if he was still around. Sometimes I imagined that he was simply away on a trip and that he would soon reappear and we would take up where we left off. The truth was, I wasn't yet ready to sever all connections with Mike; it was comforting to know that he was still having an influence on my life. Although consciously I acknowledged that he was dead, perhaps unconsciously I was still trying to deny this reality.

I continued attending the McMaster University IVCF area committee meetings, and continued to identify with Mike's work with the students. At the next meeting there was a discussion about ways in which we, as adult supporters, could assist the students until a new staff worker came on the scene. Several of us offered to attend the student meetings, and to be available as a support to the students. We all felt that the work must go on; we were a close group and it was lovely to enjoy their fellowship and friendship.

In February, about a month after Mike's death, I was invited by Mike's boss, Don, to attend a staff meeting at which Dr John Stott from England would be present, for an informal question-and-answer period. Dr Stott was coming over for the 60th Anniversary celebrations of IVCF in Canada.

I was pleased that they had invited me – that I was still included as an IVCF supporter. Yet when I arrived at this staff meeting, I felt somewhat self-conscious. In the end, I decided to sit near the back where I would be relatively inconspicuous, and able to slip out discreetly if I became emotional. Throughout the meeting, I was very conscious of Mike's absence. Nevertheless, it was a privilege to sit and listen to the man who had been instrumental in launching me forward in my Christian walk nearly ten years before. I was impressed by his wisdom and candour, and also his graciousness and humility.

Don had spoken to Dr Stott about the accident, as it was such a fresh tragedy in the life of IVCF, and Dr Stott opened the discussion with expressions of condolence at the loss of their staff worker and one of the students. The following discussion was informal and candid. Staff were encouraged to ask Dr Stott anything they wished – and they did. Many asked about the work of IVCF in England, and the Institute for Contemporary Christianity in London, where Dr Stott taught. Dr Stott was gracious and responsive in answering all the questions. And just as Dr Stott had impressed me all those many years before, I was again moved and inspired by his manner.

After the meeting, I was introduced to Dr Stott, and he signed a couple of books that I had brought with me. In the front cover of his most recent book, he wrote: 'It has been special to meet you at this time', and wrote out the following verse from Jeremiah 29:11: '"For I know the plans I have for you," declares the Lord, "plans to prosper you and not to harm you, plans to give you a hope and a future."'

This promise from the Bible gave me further courage and determination to press on; but Mike was still so much a part of me, and I wanted to maintain links with him, his work, his family and his friends, many of whom had become mutual friends of mine too. I still felt safer with people who had known Mike, rather than having to explain my situation to people who didn't know.

About a month after Mike died, Mike's parents held a thanksgiving/memorial service for him at their local church in England. I was unable to go, but Mike's family sent me an audiotape of the service. Several hundred people from all over Britain attended, including many of Mike's school and university friends. Once again, Mike's family participated in what must have been a deeply moving and poignant service. David read the Scripture lesson; Maggie played her flute; Ann read a poem; Douglas spoke, and Alan Walker, a fellow missionary with them in Uganda, gave the address. I was encouraged to hear that they were being cared for by God as I was.

There was a young woman in my church who was looking for some lodgings, while she worked as an occupational therapist at a local hospital. As I had a spare room, it worked out well for her to stay with me. Carol was tall with short dark hair, tapered at the nape of her neck. She was a keen Christian, and anxious to live out her Christian faith in all areas of her life. She was wonderful company for me around the house, and it was useful to have some extra monthly income to go towards my mortgage payments. We shared all the facilities of the house, and sometimes we had meals together. Her schedule was so busy that we didn't always see a lot of each other, but it was nice to know there was someone around.

In March, Don Posterski came with another IVCF staff member to clear out Mike's office. It was a help to have Mike's downstairs office cleaned out to make more room for my lodger, but it forced me to face Mike's death still further. It was so hard to watch them empty all his files, saving only a few documents of current importance, and throwing out the rest. They filled more than a whole black plastic sackful – all his work records and camp and IVCF resource materials. Three years of work was in one afternoon dumped in the dustbin. I could tell that it was very hard for Don too.

Fortunately, I had the spring and summer off work, so, without being consciously aware that I was doing so, I embarked on a type of pilgrimage: to revisit places where Mike and I had been, to get together with family and friends who knew him. Instinctively, I sensed a need to go back through our life together, before I could move forward without him.

My first trip was a return to Ottawa where Mike and

I had met, studied together, become engaged, and spent the first year of our marriage. The daffodils were in early bloom, poking through the wet snow that was still lying about in patches. My grandparents were happy to have James and me visit for a fortnight. I walked to Carleton University and wandered around the campus, recalling the many happy times we spent together there. The geography department and Mike's postgraduate reading room were still much the same. The cafeteria that led out to a patio on the river reminded me of the many times we had eaten our lunch outside. There were a few students milling about, although it was fairly quiet, as it was half-term and most would have been studying for their exams. The quietness reflected my emptiness within. In some ways, it felt much the same; but in other ways, it felt totally different.

After my tour of the university, I rang up some former student friends and Mike's professors. First I went to see Margo, the Carleton VCF student with whom I had shared a one-to-one Bible study for a year. She greeted me with a smile and a hug. 'Catherine, it is so good to see you. How are you?' she asked.

'I'm fine – gradually moving forward. How about you? Thank you so much for coming to Mike's funeral. I was amazed to see so many from Ottawa.'

'I nearly didn't come – I couldn't believe it. I didn't want it to be Mike. A friend finally persuaded me to come.' Tears came to her eyes, and I looked at her closely.

'Margo, I know how fond you were of Mike. He cared for you a lot too. He treasured the pencilled drawing of Beethoven you did for him – it's still up in his office.'

She smiled through her tears, and we embraced once again, sharing our mutual loss.

With a sniff she stepped back and spoke once more. 'Catherine, I've thought a lot about you over the last few months. Do you remember saying to me, when we had those Bible studies, that as much as you would never want Mike to die, you believed that you would be OK because God would still be with you, and your relationship with him should be primary?'

I looked thoughtfully at her for a while. 'Now you mention it, I do remember saying something like that. But it never occurred to me that it would actually happen. I know I must put God first above everything else – yet I loved Mike so much. But God is still with me, and I'm trying to trust that he will work things for good. It's so hard, though. Even with God's help, I sometimes wonder how I can go on without Mike. I can't imagine how someone who isn't a Christian could cope.'

I thought about what Margo said on my way home. Did I love Mike *too much*? I loved him as much as a woman could love a man, yet I didn't *own* him – I had to share him with many other people. Perhaps it was our busy lives that helped me not to become too possessive, and which might now be helping me in my grief.

Other friends of Mike's were equally warm and welcoming as we shared some of our memories of him. They gave me encouragement in their kindness and support, but our visits were tinged with sadness as I recognised that the days we had spent together were now over.

One afternoon I drove back along the canal where we had spent many winter evenings skating, and where Mike had proposed to me. I retraced the cycle paths we had frequently used. Each time I retraced our steps, a different memory was sparked – and the stab of his loss would once again pierce my heart.

By now, James was four months old, and seemed to be constantly hungry. My grandparents suggested buying him some baby cereal, and his very proud great-grandad fed him his first solid food. As I looked on as a protective new mother, it occurred to me that this was the first of many milestones that James would have that Mike would not be here to celebrate with me.

One couple that I was particularly keen to meet up with was John and Debbie Bowen. John had been Mike's supervisor, and Mike and I had spent many hours with them and their son and daughter, now well into their school years, when we lived in Ottawa. John and Debbie were pleased to see James for the first time, and we caught up on the news of mutual friends and acquaintances, and reminisced about our days in the Carleton VCF. Together we remembered previous summers at camp, and I recalled how Mike and I had been planning to go to camp together as a family this summer. 'Why don't you come anyway?' asked John. 'James could be looked after by a babysitter there, and we would be happy to have you as camp counsellor in the LIT [Leaders in Training] programme.' It was a kind and generous invitation, and I was pleased to accept. It would be one more plan of Mike's that I could bring to fruition, and another place of warm memories of Mike to which I could return.

Soon I was back at home again in Hamilton, and looking forward to James's and my trip to England towards the end of April, when I would again see Mike's parents and meet up with some of his friends. In another of God's gracious provisions, my father gave James and me a gift of free return air fares to Britain, which he was able to obtain through his frequent-flyer scheme from business flights. It was a new experience for me to travel for eight hours on my own with a baby to look after, but thankfully James slept most of the way and we arrived without mishap.

Our plane landed in Edinburgh, where we were to attend the wedding of one of Mike's friends, John, who had been one of the ushers at our wedding. He was to marry a girl called Anne. We stayed with my father's brother, Uncle Billy, and Aunt Maud for the weekend, and afterwards planned to drive down to the south of England with Bob and Sue, some dear friends. My aunt and uncle, themselves grandparents of two little boys, looked after James for me while I went to the wedding with my friends.

The sky was a dreary grey, typical of April weather in Edinburgh, but between shower bursts there were one or two glimpses of sunshine and the wedding was a happy and joyful occasion. This was the second wedding I had been to since Mike's death, and again I felt somewhat self-conscious. Not many at the wedding knew me, but I was painfully aware of being one of only a few single people there, and felt a bit awkward at not having a partner for the dance afterwards. However, my friends refused to let me be a wallflower, and in spite of myself I had fun. Anne looked lovely, her slim waist showed off to effect in a full-length white gown. I was happy for John; they seemed well suited to each other.

Early on Monday morning, Bob and Sue, along with their one-year-old son, Andrew, came to collect James and me from my uncle's and aunt's home and we set off on the long drive down to the south of England. We drove via Durham, so that I could visit Durham University where Mike and Bob studied together. Several times during our relationship Mike had shown me pictures of the university, and had spoken fondly of his time there. He had told me he wanted to take me there one day, so it was a special privilege to see it now.

The sky had cleared of the dark grey clouds, and although the morning mist had not yet fully lifted, we could see the cathedral spire as we neared this lovely university. The university and adjoining cathedral seemed peaceful and idyllic, hidden among trees and shrubs and surrounded by a flowing river; the campus was cut off from the hustle and bustle of the city on an island of its own. I could picture Mike in such a lovely setting, studying – but also larking about with his friends in a punt on the river.

We stood on the arching stone bridge linking the university to the town, and gazed upon this picture-postcard scene. The dew on the ground and the frost on the trees were sparkling like thousands of ice-diamonds as the sun rose, barely able to melt them in its weak and watery warmth. Our breath puffed out like smoke in the chilly air, and I bundled James up warmly as we pushed our babies in pushchairs around the university campus. It was a lovely sight, but the morning sunlight of early spring wasn't quite strong enough to cut through the chill in the air.

We wandered around St John's College where Mike had read geography, and Bob showed me the vicar's home where he and Mike had taken up residence during their student days. We entered the famous cathedral and marvelled at the intricate detail of the stonework and the tremendous height of the ceiling. The stained-glass windows were brilliant against the sun, and gave the impression that God was sending his light and colour into the old building. In the midst of my awe at the beauty and the majesty, I was overwhelmed with a deep sadness. It should have been Mike showing me around his old alma mater.

As I looked at the various memorial windows and tombstones placed in memory of loved ones situated at various locations throughout the cathedral, I was struck by my own mortality. Many generations had come and gone since this cathedral was built, and in all likelihood it would still be standing after many more generations had passed away. I turned to Bob and voiced my thoughts, 'It's amazing to think of the history of previous generations who worshipped here. Soon that's all that will be left of us too; we'll be just another name on a tombstone – although probably not in such an auspicious place as this!'

'I was thinking that too,' Bob replied. 'Death is the one certainty of life, isn't it?' Slowly he continued, 'You're thinking of Mike, aren't you? I still find it hard to think of him in the past tense, dead and gone like these people of long ago. It seemed only like yesterday when we came to church here, studied and joked about. A day hasn't gone by since I haven't thought about him, and how hard it must be for you without him.' I smiled in response. 'Thanks,' I said, and we hugged in remembrance of our mutual loss. The ice in my chest thawed a little in the warmth of Bob's and Sue's friendship.

By now, our sons were becoming restless at our adult reminiscences, so we piled back into the car and drove the rest of the way down to Margate where Mike's parents, Douglas and Ann, were waiting for us with a welcoming coal fire burning in their sitting-room and a delicious hot meal on the table. It felt cosy and safe to be among Mike's family and friends.

The rains of April finally gave way to the gentle warmth of May sunshine, and Mike's parents took Maggie, James and me for a lovely holiday in the New Forest. Soon after this, the whole Hare household was involved in the last-minute preparations for Maggie's wedding, and the week before that, Douglas, as lay minister of Holy Trinity Church, was going to baptise James.

The baptism was a special ceremony held at the early family service on a Sunday morning. My sister Fiona's friend in Alabama had hand-sewn a delicate old-fashioned christening gown, and Fiona had embroidered his name and the date on it. It was intricate, but not feminine; it had fine pleats and embroidery on the front. Fortunately, my father was over in Britain on business, and so was also able to come. Douglas, dressed in his priestly garb, proudly made the sign of the cross on little James's high forehead. Others in the congregation knew how special an occasion it was for us, and sent cards and gifts for James. It was another event that Mike and I had planned before his death, and so I was pleased to be able to fulfil one more of his wishes.

Maggie's wedding was the climax of a beautiful holiday, held on a glorious day in May. The only slight shadow over the sunny day was of course the absence of Mike. It was a happy occasion nevertheless. In the midst of the joy and celebration, and filled with the warmth and love of family and friends, almost imperceptibly my mood lifted slightly. I was able to be sincerely happy for Maggie and to wish her well in her marriage to Chris.

When we returned to Canada, summer was coming into full bloom. As the weather continued to improve, so also did my spirits, and I tackled caring for a household and looking after James with renewed energy and enthusiasm. Gradually I was gaining confidence as I became accustomed to the constant responsibility of parenting and looking after things on my own. As yet, I still couldn't see very far ahead, but I was now beginning to be able to plan and think ahead a month or two, whereas before I was just existing from day to day. It was a help to have camp and the cottage to look forward to later in the summer.

Friends found a babysitter for me to assist with James's care at camp, and so in due course the three of us set off in my car, heavy laden with sleeping bags, suitcases and all the paraphernalia a baby needs: playpen, milk formula, toys, nappies and teddy bear. My heart ached to return to a place that had meant so much to Mike, and where he had excelled in his gifts and abilities.

At one group meeting at camp there was a discussion about God's power, and the leader asked if anyone had experienced God's power in a personal way. One camper said she had seen God's power earlier in the year as her friend was healed of cancer. Another lad said he had seen God's power as demonstrated in the transformed life of his brother, who had been a drug addict and who had now been rehabilitated. Others recounted equally miraculous events in their lives of healings, and even a resuscitation back to life after a near-drowning. Hesistantly, I raised my hand; I too had experienced God's power. It wasn't as dramatic or as visible a miracle, but I realised that it was evidence of God's working nevertheless. I spoke up: 'Sometimes God's power can be demonstrated in small and quiet ways as well. The fact that I am able to be here this year without Mike is one example. On my own, I don't know how I would have coped without Mike, but God is giving me the strength to carry on without him.' In fact, perhaps the greatest miracle of all is not outward physical healing, but the inner transformation of people's hearts and minds as they turn to him.

John and Debbie Bowen and I spent many hours talking about Mike and his death, and where we saw God in all of this. John noticed my continued interest in – and enjoyment of – camp and IVCF, and asked me if I had ever considered becoming an IVCF staff worker myself. Later, I walked around the camp while pondering on this possibility. For a long time I had wanted to work more directly in Christian ministry of some sort or other, and helping Mike had partly fulfilled this desire. I knew that working in full-time ministry with the students would fulfil a deep personal sense of calling, and I believed it would be a rewarding and fulfilling vocation.

The high point of camp for me was the last of John's 'Building Blocks' lectures. He spoke about the biblical picture of heaven, and pointed out that – contrary to commonly held beliefs – heaven as portrayed in the Bible isn't a return to the garden of paradise, but instead an entrance into a lively and active, creative and productive new city. With cartoon pictures, he dispelled many of our myths of heaven, such as the place where we sit, with golden wings, on fluffy clouds playing harps for eternity. Or perhaps an even less appealing picture – that of an eternal church service where we have to sit passively for hours and hours on end!

This was revolutionary new thinking for me, and I wondered what Mike might be doing with God. Could he see me? Or was he so busy in a different realm that he had no awareness of us on earth? I recalled a comment made by one of the students in the accident, when I asked her how it happened. She said that Mike had been joking in the van as they travelled on their way, as was his wont, and just before the crash had asked, 'Do you think there could be skiing in heaven?' Perhaps he did go skiing that day after all.

After the session, I went up to John and said, 'Thanks, John. You make heaven seem a lot more exciting and interesting than I had ever before imagined.'

John replied, 'Yes, I believe it will exceed all our expectations. Come out on a canoe trip with me after lunch and we can talk.'

Later that afternoon, John and I stepped into a canoe and pushed it out on to the calm fresh lake around which the camps were built. For a little while, we hunted for a water snake that someone had spied near some rocks by the shore. It was quiet on the lake as we dipped our paddles in unison. We heard birds twittering in the distance, and were pleased to spot a pair of loons, diving underwater for fish.

Finally, I broke the silence and said, 'John, it's so lovely and peaceful here – perhaps this is a glimpse of heaven.'

He nodded in agreement. 'Yes, it is beautiful, so restful and quiet. It's a lovely spot to get in touch with our Creator.'

I persisted. 'You know, John, ever since Mike died, I've wondered a lot about what heaven is really like – but the Bible doesn't really say much about it, does it?'

John thought for a moment, then explained, 'It gives us pictures and images, but we can only understand it in terms of our own earthly experience. We'll only know fully how wonderful it is when we get there ourselves.'

'I suppose so, yet I wish it said more. John, something bothers me. I mean, I know that there will be no more tears or mourning there, and I do believe that I will meet Mike again, but we won't be married, will we? We'll never be a couple again.'

'No, perhaps not,' John responded, 'not in the way we are married here on earth, yet I believe that what we experience here is a foretaste of heaven. Even the most fulfilling sexual intercourse here on earth doesn't bring perfect intimacy and unity. I don't believe heaven will be in any way less than or inferior to life on earth; it will be much more, not less. Perhaps there we will find deeper intimacy and a grander unity and oneness with each other than we can experience here.'

I let his words sink into my mind. 'Hmm. I hadn't thought of it that way before. C. S. Lewis says that our life here on earth is merely "shadowlands" – and that heaven is more clear and vivid, more real than life on earth. I certainly hope so.'

The sun dropped down behind the trees, casting long shadows on the lake. We realised that it must be nearly suppertime, so we paddled towards the shore so that we had time to change before we ate.

The LIT programme soon came to an end, and the campers were duly awarded the certificates that granted them status as camp counsellors, and James and I returned home to the city once more. We weren't back in Hamilton for long before we had to pack up again to go to my grandparents' cottage at Georgian Bay. My brother, David, and

Robin and little Ben came with us. Here was another place of strong memories of Mike. We had spent our honeymoon at the cottage, had fun-filled holidays with family and friends and, perhaps most difficult of all, it was the last place that I had seen Mike alive. I expected it to be really hard to go back to the place where Mike had had his accident, but in reality it wasn't as bad as I'd feared. Other happy childhood memories of our summer home crowded in among the poignant memories of Mike, and I didn't sit around moping for long. We easily filled the warm sunny days with swimming, boating, water-skiing and playing tennis. The children had great fun splashing in the paddling pool and playing in the sandpit.

Occasionally, I would think of Mike when relaxing while reading, or lazing about on the beach. One afternoon, when I looked out across the bay, I recalled the view I'd had on that fateful morning. Yet it was so different now. The sun was warm and the water peaceful, with little ripples of happiness before the evening calm. The accident began to seem a long time ago. Had it only been eight months? In some ways, it seemed just like yesterday, but so much had happened in the intervening time that in other ways it seemed like a lifetime ago.

As the summer drew to a close, I reflected on my pilgrimage over the previous months and could see that I had made some progress forward in my journey of grief. Each time I had returned to a place of remembrance, the pain of the loss hurt, but it hadn't entirely overwhelmed me as I had feared it might; on the contrary, and to my surprise, it actually seemed to ease the pain – as if by walking through it, it lost its power over me. Facing the fact of Mike's death head on helped me move forward in the process of mourning, rather than trying to deny it by pretending that it hadn't happened. It was similar in talking about Mike and his death. At first it was hard to talk about it without crying or a lump coming to my throat, but gradually, with practice, it became easier, until soon I found I could speak about him with equanimity, naturally and freely as he came to mind.

Summer soon came to an end, and I knew that I needed to decide what I was going to do in the autumn. My maternity leave was due to terminate at the end of August, and my supervisor and I made arrangements for my return to work. This would be part time on a new ward. I suddenly wondered whether I should go forward with my original plans, or whether I should pursue a completely different course of action now that my life had changed so drastically.

John's suggestion at camp that I consider working for IVCF was often in my thoughts. I thought of Elizabeth Elliot, who had lost her husband to the Auca Indians, but who still went out there as a missionary herself. I hadn't been officially appointed with Mike, but his calling had become my calling, and we shared a love for the students and a respect and admiration for the work of IVCF. I knew I was well qualified for the job, having a Master of Theological Studies degree and having had some work experience in Christian ministry. I had worked with the poor at Yonge Street Mission, worked as a short-term missionary in southern Thailand, and served as chaplain in a hospital. I had also been directly involved with Mike in his work at the universities, occasionally attending meetings and often having the students over to our home. And more recently, I'd helped out at their summer camps. In addition, I believed that many of Mike's financial and prayer supporters would be willing to transfer their support to me, as many of them were my friends as well. On the face of it, it seemed an ideal plan.

No one else had as yet come forward to replace Mike, so I enquired about the post. I sent a letter and a copy of my CV to Don Posterski and he telephoned me to invite me to his home in Toronto. My parents agreed to look after James for me, so I made the hour-long drive into the big city.

As ever, Don welcomed me warmly as I entered the house. 'How are you, Lady Catherine? It was good to see you at camp in the summer.'

'Fine, thanks,' I replied. 'It has been hard, but I believe I am gradually moving forward on my own – and James is great.'

He looked closely at me and responded, 'You do look well. You have coped remarkably well since the loss of Mike. We're proud of you.' He and I walked into the sitting-room where we sat down, and Don's wife, Beth, brought us each a cup of coffee.

Don continued. 'Catherine, to get down to business. I have read your letter and carefully reviewed your CV. You undoubtedly have the qualifications and experience in ministry and your interest and involvement with IVCF for me to consider you for a staff position.' He paused. 'However, I must be honest with you and say that I do not think it would be right for you to take over Mike's position at this time. You are just too close to the situation. I can see how you would like to carry on his work, but you wouldn't be able to do it the same way that he did.' He smiled apologetically as he said these difficult words, which he knew would disappoint me.

I let his words sink in for a moment. They were so unexpected; it was indeed a deep disappointment. Tentatively I began, 'I agree that I am close to the situation, but I'm not sure why you think it is a problem that I would be different. Yes, I have different gifts and a different personality, yet anyone else would do it differently from Mike. I realise Mike was unique.'

'You would be put in an awkward and difficult position,' Don responded, 'because there would be expectations impossible for anyone to reach. Catherine, I'm sorry to have to say this to you. I would be delighted to appoint you to a staff position at some point, but not at this time, not this location. If you are still interested in IVCF work in the next couple of years, then why don't you come back to me then, and we could see if there are some other universities where you could work?' Don made it very clear that he strongly felt it would not be right.

Tears came to my eyes as I drove back to Hamilton. I couldn't quite understand his reasoning, and I was disappointed that he would not give me a chance. It was true that I had wanted to carry on Mike's vision and his work, but I did recognise that of course I would do things differently from him. Mike had better organisational skills than me – although I would have put greater emphasis on counselling and nurturing of the students. But now my dream-bubble, before it even had a chance to take off, had burst. I telephoned John Bowen, to let him know of the outcome of our interview. He said he would be happy to chat with me at the staff conference at camp, to be held in a few weeks' time.

There were two other women who had also been involved in helping the McMaster VCF since Mike died, and the three of us drove north to the camps together. We enjoyed the fellowship of the other staff workers and the freshness of the outdoors, going on walks in the wood, and learning from the interesting Bible teaching given by Gordon MacDonald, who had come all the way from America to be key speaker at the event.

John and I had some time to talk that evening while we had our before-bedtime snack. He took me aside and said, 'Catherine, I'm sorry to hear that Don doesn't feel that it is right for you to take over Mike's position. You know, when I asked you if you had ever considered becoming a staff worker, I wasn't particularly thinking about Mike's position. Perhaps there is something else for you.'

'Perhaps,' I replied. 'Don said that too; he agreed that I was well qualified, but he just didn't think it would be wise for me to take on Mike's position because I was too close to the situation. To be honest, I don't quite understand his reasoning, but I accept his decision.'

John then said, 'You might like to talk to Jim or some other staff here this weekend, who might help you understand.'

On the Sunday morning, I approached Jim Berney, National Director of IVCF-Canada. Jim had discussed with Don the possibility of my employment, and had listened to Don's position on the matter. 'Catherine, Don may or may not have clearly defined reasons, but he obviously has a strong gut feeling that it would not be the right course of action. He has good judgment in these matters.'

'Fair enough,' I replied. 'I suppose I will just have to wait and see the way forward from here.'

Jim Berney encouraged me, 'You are still in our prayers, Catherine. I know God will lead you.'

Thoughtfully, I walked towards the chalet where everyone was congregating for a final worship time together before we packed up to drive home. John and I sat beside each other near the back and joined wholeheartedly in the singing of camp and worship songs. Suddenly, they started singing 'Shine, Jesus, Shine', the chorus to 'Lord, the Light of your Love' by Graham Kendrick, which Mike had introduced to the camp by bringing it over from England a couple of years before. A catch came to my voice – I couldn't continue singing. John noticed my silence, and stopped himself; it had reminded him of Mike as well. When the song ended, we embraced, both freely crying over our loss. 'You know, Catherine, I really loved Mike. I wish I'd had a chance to tell him,' he whispered in my ear.

I responded. 'He knew that. He loved you too. He told

me how whenever there was a staff get-together he always found himself congregating near you.'

We both knew that those days were over. Mike's IVCF work was over, and *I* couldn't keep it alive. It hurt, but I realised that someone else would need to replace him and carry on the work – in a different manner, with a different vision.

Painful as it was, I would have to let go of Mike – his work, as well as him as a person and the life we shared together. I would always treasure my memories of him, but that was what they must now become – memories. I couldn't hold on to the past; I needed to move forward, on my own, to find my own identity and calling. Yet I was comforted by the fact that I knew I wasn't alone. The Lord was beside me, and behind me, and ahead of me, all the while leading the way.

8

Letting Go

'A father to the fatherless, a defender of widows,
is God in his holy dwelling' (Psalm 68:5).

Now that the door of working with IVCF had clearly shut,
I reconsidered my original plan of returning to work as a
medical social worker. Someone had once said to me that
it was unwise for a person who has suffered a deep loss,
such as the death of a spouse, to make any major decisions
or changes for at least a year. I couldn't remember when
or where I had heard this, perhaps during my social-work
training, but it did seem to make sense. There was no rush
to make drastic changes in my lifestyle – the loss of Mike
himself was more than enough. I was settled in the area,
had a child to care for, had friends and family nearby, an
interesting and rewarding job, and a regular income.

Before James was born I had worked full time. I was
pleased that now a part-time social-work job opened up at
the hospital. This meant I had time to spend with James, as
well as run the house on my own. Work kept me active so
that I couldn't wallow in self-pity, and the part-time hours
enabled me to look after James and the house.

My new appointment was on a medical ward, primarily
serving elderly people who had suffered strokes or broken
hips, or other ailments serious enough to require hospi-
talisation. My role was to provide emotional support to

patients and their families while they were in hospital, and to liaise with community services when the patients were discharged from hospital.

It was quite a contrast to the maternity ward. There, the focus was on the joy and anticipation at the beginning of life; here, elderly patients were waiting for death. I found it depressing to see senior citizens ill and in pain; some with no family members to visit; some with no home to go to. I could see that many people were far worse off than myself. I was thankful for the blessings of a lovely son, a good job and kind friends and family.

One woman in particular drew my attention. She was only sixty-five and she had been admitted to hospital with a malignant brain tumour. The cancer had progressed quickly, and her prognosis was poor. The doctors gave her chemotherapy and radiotherapy, but these treatments failed to arrest the relentless growth of the tumour. At each setback and disappointment, she and I would talk about her dashed hopes and expectations. We talked about her recent retirement from office work, and how she was looking forward to a time of rest and relaxation with her husband. But her serious illness deprived her of these days that she had so looked forward to.

When it became clear that she didn't have long to live, we talked about her readiness for death. Had she put her financial affairs in order? Could she talk about her illness and imminent death with her family? Had she expressed her wishes concerning her belongings, her funeral and burial to her family? Was she at peace with God?

It was hard to face all these issues, yet with my own experience of loss, I had some understanding of the sensitivity needed. I remembered how helpful I had found it to talk about my situation. It gave me courage to broach some of these difficult subjects with her. Her husband and family were reluctant to face her imminent death, and at times she felt frustrated because they didn't want to talk about it.

When the time came for her to say goodbye, I was able to encourage her and her husband to take the opportunity to express their feelings to one another. It was a particularly poignant moment for me as I recalled how much it hurt that I never had the chance to say goodbye to Mike before he died. Her husband was grateful to be with her when she died, and afterwards we sat together while he waited for their daughter and family to arrive. He shed tears of sadness and grief, and expressed his feelings of emptiness and the sudden loss of purpose at her departure.

As a widow myself, I knew that I was not entirely detached and objective in my work with these people. Having experienced such a loss myself helped me sympathise in a deeper way, yet – surprisingly – I was able to remain calm and composed when they were upset and anxious. All those times talking with my family members and friends helped me talk about death with others more openly and directly.

My own sadness at this particular patient's death was tempered by the awareness that I had in some small way assisted in her preparation for this event. And, in a special way, helping her took me a step further along my own path of grief. The truth of the verse 'He who refreshes others will himself be refreshed' (Proverbs 11:25) became true for me. The rewarding work of consoling and encouraging others didn't provide an explanation as to why Mike had died, but it did alleviate some of my own sorrow and perplexity, and it gave some meaning to what otherwise seemed to be meaningless. My bereavement prepared me for ministering to others in a similar situation. I am certain that I would not have become as involved with this woman and her family if I myself had not experienced the loss of my husband.

Thus my work at the hospital, although at times emotionally draining, was interesting and rewarding; it gave added focus and structure to my life, in addition to my role as a single parent. I was fortunate in that a neighbour was able to look after James while I was at work.

Carol, my lodger, was still sharing the house, and she was good company. It helped having another adult to talk to, and to discuss the events of the day over a meal together. James was now sitting up in a high chair, and so was able to sit at table with us. I still breastfed him for some feeds, but he also drank milk from a bottle for part of the time, which gave me greater freedom to leave him with someone else for a while. On one occasion when Carol and I were chatting while we sat down to tea, I fed James his bottle at the same time. I was becoming quite adept at doing at least two things at once these days – even my reflexes were improving as I caught things in mid-air that James dropped!

Carol and I started to have a serious conversation about our respective jobs – occupational therapist and social worker. We were becoming quite intense, when suddenly Carol burst out laughing and pointed at James. When I looked at him, I saw that the oriface into which I had plugged the nipple of his bottle was not, as I had thought, his mouth, but was in fact his ear! He hadn't made a sound, but was just sitting there looking at me quizzically. I burst into laughter too. Despite the difficulties, life wasn't all sorrow and sadness, nor all work and seriousness.

Yet there seemed to be so many challenges in having the full responsibility of running a home. I resented mowing the lawn and taking out the rubbish – these had definitely been Mike's jobs, and I had no desire to take them on! On one occasion I was particularly repulsed when I lifted up the black sacks to carry them round to the front of the house for the dustman, only to discover that they were covered in giant slugs. I screamed as I accidentally touched one of these slimy creatures, dropped the sack, and was tempted to leave it for someone else when I suddenly realised that there was no one else to do it. Mike was no longer here to remove unwanted mini-beasts such as wasps or centipedes that managed to sneak into the house. I gritted my teeth and knocked the creatures off the bags with a stick, so that I could carry the sacks round to the front. When I recovered from my revulsion, I felt some degree of pride that I had faced this particular fear, and took heart that I might be able to do other things that I had not as yet attempted on my own.

With each new task accomplished, I began to develop a sense of achievement. I was still feeling pleased with myself that I'd managed to assemble a tricycle for James, when I decided to replace the kitchen light. After lots of complications in connecting it, it finally worked – much to my pride and amazement. I boasted of my new accomplishment to my brother when he visited me. He was duly impressed, then asked, 'Did you switch off the electricity before doing this?'

I nodded, 'Yes, of course I did – I turned off the light switch as the instructions said – I'm not that stupid!'

He looked at me aghast, 'No, I mean at the *mains*!' The look on my face made it abundantly clear that I hadn't. 'You could have electrocuted yourself!' he said, a look of horror etched across his face. I had obviously been very lucky – and had learnt yet another of the many practical things still to be learnt.

The autumn passed quickly; I was asked to speak at the IVCF World Day of Prayer at my church to be held on the first Sunday of November, Remembrance Sunday. In the past it had always mildly annoyed me that IVCF held their prayer day on the first Sunday in November, because it always had to compete with all the ceremonies of remembrance, and I felt that it got largely missed in the midst. But on this occasion, it seemed fitting.

Before the service, I wrote out prayers and placed a bright red poppy on the lapel of my navy-blue suit. As I looked at the poppy, I thought of England. How I loved the poppies in the fields – but as well as being pretty flowers, they were a symbol of sorrow and loss.

When my turn came, I walked up to the podium and looked out over the sea of faces and identified my association with IVCF. 'It seems particularly appropriate that IVCF is holding their World Day of Prayer on Remembrance Sunday. I can't think of IVCF without recalling the work of my husband at McMaster and Brock universities. But since his death, the work must go on . . .'

Afterwards, several church members came up to me and said they were moved by my prayers and wanted to support IVCF. One couple said they were pleased to see that I was able to talk about Mike. They thought because I had been away so much over the past year, that I was avoiding church folk and having difficulty in facing his loss. I recognised that I had indeed been away a lot, and ought to appreciate the caring community here at the local church of which I was a part.

Someone mentioned to me that they were going to be putting small stained-glass windows in the church, and asked me if I was interested in putting some money towards one in memory of Mike. The church was only four years old, and built in the shape of a hexagon with a tall steeple in the centre. As a modern building, and in spite of the steeple, it tended to look like a large pizza parlour. Therefore I was pleased that they wanted to change the glass to stained – I felt it would help the place look more 'churchy'. It also appealed to me to identify a memorial for Mike. I had put a headstone for Mike at his burial site, but it seemed important to do something else in his memory as well. Mike's parents were having similar feelings, and had a bench placed in Mike's memory at his old school in England.

Both my family and Mike's family contributed, and we were able to purchase a small window of Mary with baby Jesus on her lap. It seemed particularly appropriate as I was left on my own with a baby. We held a ceremony during a Sunday service to dedicate the new windows. My family were pleased to have some concrete way of recognising Mike, and publicly stating how much he meant to us. It was yet another physical reminder that Mike had died, and that I needed to move on without him.

I knew that my focus had to change from Mike to James, who was now my family. James's first birthday was coming up on 16 November, and I needed to plan something for him. Now that I was on my own, anniversaries and birthdays seemed very hard. My birthday and Mike's birthday and our wedding anniversary all took place in the summer, but I had been with family members on these occasions – which made them a little easier. But no other family members were planning to visit for James's birthday, as it fell in term-time mid-week. I knew I would have to plan it on my own.

With my babysitter's help, I invited fifteen local children over for a birthday party. Being only one, James wasn't fully aware of what was going on, but the children who came were aged between three and six and enjoyed playing games and eating cake, and taking home a balloon and goody bag. We tried to teach James how to blow out his candles, and he did quite well. It struck me yet again how quickly he was growing up. He could walk now; and although he couldn't yet speak, I could tell that he understood some of the words I said to him.

The next event to which we looked forward both with happy and nervous anticipation was Christmas. It would be hard to face my first Christmas without Mike. My parents kindly invited us over to their place in Toronto

for a large family gathering. My sister and her sons
were coming up from Alabama, and my brothers and
their wives and children would be coming over. Even
my grandparents and uncle were coming down from
Ottawa.

It was like many Christmases of my childhood at my
parents' home: lots of presents and food and music, and
an evening carol service at the church. James and his
young cousins had a happy time opening their presents
and playing with one another. Yet I kept remembering
Mike, and recalling the previous year when he had been
there and James was just one month old. Mike had put a
holly bow tie around James's neck, and Mike himself had
danced around the sitting-room in some Father Christmas
boxer shorts that Maggie had sent him from England.

No one mentioned Mike, yet I knew that other family
members were thinking about him too. It seemed important to acknowledge him in some way without detracting
from the happiness of the occasion, so I reinstated an
old family tradition. After a delicious turkey dinner and
followed by traditional Christmas pudding, we drank
some sparkling wine – a special Christmas treat. In
the past, Grandad or some other senior member of the
family would raise a glass and toast first the queen and
then absent family and friends. I raised my glass to make
these toasts, and mentioned Mike as an absent family
member. Most of us had tears in our eyes, but it felt like
a meaningful gesture and helped me to voice aloud what
I knew we were all thinking.

The New Year brought with it new challenges and steps
forward. The date of 16 January was the anniversary of
Mike's death, and I knew that I needed to acknowledge
this day in some way. I had taken an extended holiday
from work, so I decided to take James to England to visit
Mike's parents.

We spent two to three happy weeks there visiting

family and friends. Chris and Maggie came down, and they stayed for a few days as well. We toured some local sights, an oast house, a windmill, and we took James to an indoor swimming pool. As we drove along the country lanes of Kent, passing little cottages, pubs and fields of sheep, a deep longing came over me. 'I love England,' I exclaimed to Chris and Maggie. 'Mike wanted to come back here. The only reason we didn't was because he couldn't find work here. I wish I could stay.'

Chris glanced back over his shoulder, 'Are you sure you aren't trying to find Mike?' He pulled me up with a start. 'Maybe,' I replied thoughtfully, and wondered at the truth of this possibility. Perhaps I was still searching for Mike. I recalled the time when I saw someone in an orange anorak with a tweed cap riding a bicycle down the road and I took a double take, thinking for an instant it was Mike. Could this feeling of expectancy and waiting be me trying to bring him back?

We regularly went for walks on the beach. The air was bracing in the winter, but the freshness of the sea helped blow the cobwebs of self-pity away. Maggie and I walked side by side along on the sand, while Chris ran ahead with James.

'How are you, now that a year has gone past?' Maggie asked gently.

'On the whole, I think I am doing OK,' I replied. 'It was helpful to go back and visit all the people Mike and I knew, and now that I am back at work, we're getting into a routine.'

Maggie nodded in understanding. 'Me too. I enjoy my teaching, and Chris is wonderful, but I still miss Mike terribly.'

I nodded in agreement. A thought suddenly occurred to me: 'I don't know if I can say my faith has deepened since Mike's death, but it's still there. I've made it through the past year a lot better than I thought I could.'

Mike's parents decided to have a little service of remembrance for Michael on the anniversary of his death. Mike's brother, David, and his wife, Carolyn, came, along with their two sons. On the day, the whole family walked into St Mary's chapel, a little chapel on the side of the large sanctuary of Mike's parents' church. Douglas led with a short meditation and a prayer. The rest of us sat in the pews and listened to his words. After about ten minutes, the three young boys became bored, and started running up and down the aisle. They giggled and chased one another in and out of the pews. This distraction was sufficient to bring the service to an abrupt halt, as Carolyn and I ran off to chase after our wayward rascals. Upon my return, Mike's mother looked at me with a smile. 'Oh well, Mike would understand, wouldn't he, he wasn't one for staying solemn for long.' I smiled at her in agreement.

Once back in Canada, I learned of a new part-time social-work post in the outpatient psychiatric unit. It sounded like an interesting job, so I transferred to this new area of social work. It took a little while to learn my new role, but I found it challenging and stimulating. The staff team were friendly and helpful as I learned about psychiatric illness, particularly depression and anxiety, the unit to which I was assigned. One nurse, Gloria, became a friend, and we often had lunch together. She taught me much from her wealth of ten years' experience.

Home life was equally challenging as James was climbing and toddling about and getting into things now. He was curious and happy and a constant source of delight, yet requiring full-time supervision and attention. He was a lot of work, and yet generally a very happy and healthy baby; I felt quite pleased that we were managing so well.

Having said that, I had quite a few domestic calamities at that time – on one occasion the central heating system broke down (no small matter at −20 C with a baby in the house); another time the freezer went wrong, and I returned from a weekend away to find a dreadful smell of rotting meat, and several inches of melted ice and blood floating around in the freezer. I also had burst pipes and flooding, and on another occasion I had water seepage in the kitchen which shorted out half the wiring in the house, and resulted in my needing completely new wiring.

I recounted my many tales of woe to my work-mates, and together we laughed at the combination of calamities. My supervisor then came up with the helpful suggestion that I might be covered by insurance for some of this work. Fortunately, she was correct, and it transpired that I could claim back some of the costs.

It was a new experience for me to have to call in all these various maintenance people, especially as the financial costs seemed so high. Suddenly I felt helpless and vulnerable again; my new sense of capability plummeted. These areas were definitely out of my league and I knew I needed help. It all seemed so unfair! Why wasn't Mike around to take care of these things? Yet, as I sat and thought about it rationally, I had to admit that Mike, as a geographer and book person, was not especially handy around the house either; and that, in most of these calamities, he would have had to call in outside help just as I did. It was easy to fall into the trap of assuming that all these things were much worse because Mike wasn't there.

From a distance, I could laugh at these various 'challenges', yet it caused me to do some more thinking. Each time something happened, I felt so surprised – as if I now expected God to protect me from all harm and difficulty, since I had already coped with such a difficult hardship as the loss of my husband. Two lessons were impressing themselves upon me. First, just because I had experienced one hardship did not automatically mean that I would be spared others. There wasn't necessarily an equal portion of suffering dished out to people. I thought of the mentally handicapped people I had worked with in a group home, and knew that often they had further burdens to bear, over and above their intellectual limitations. They often also had to deal with unemployment and poverty, the cruel teasing and mocking from other people, and other medical problems as well. Life isn't fair, and we can't pretend that it is.

Secondly, even though I had experienced a severe hardship, I still held this notion that God would never let something awful happen to me. I assumed that because I was one of his children, he was automatically protecting me. But God doesn't have favourites – I needed to face reality. Jesus did say, 'In this world you will have trouble. But take heart! I have overcome the world' (John 16:33). I realised there was a difference between having trust in any circumstance to the passive presumption that God would look after everything. Being a Christian did not guarantee me immunity from troubles. Jesus never promised that life would be easy, only that God is with us.

Each hurdle that I overcame gave me the courage to face the next. Very slowly, I came to believe that I actually *could* manage without Mike, albeit with the help of family and friends. 'Super mum' I was not; I couldn't do everything, but I could cook and clean, look after James, and provide for us financially. The stubborn side of me wanted to do as much as I was able to myself, but I knew also I needed to humbly accept help from others when my own resources and capabilities were exhausted. It was a delicate balance to find my own independence, and yet to accept assistance when it was needed.

Very slowly, I began to develop a sense of competence and a burgeoning self-confidence in my own identity as a widow and a single parent. Work was generally satisfying and socially stimulating, and James was a source of pride and delight. Household chores were mostly routine, but I could manage them. Life at last seemed to be going roughly OK.

But was this all there was? Was my life going to remain like this for the next twenty or thirty years? A restlessness pervaded my existence. There must be more to going to work and coming home to housework and caring for an infant. It was interesting, but routine, and I found myself missing something – someone – and with a feeling of vague anxiety and lack of fulfilment. It was almost as if I was in a state of waiting, but for what I did not know. C. S. Lewis described this feeling in his book called *A Grief Observed*: 'And grief still feels like fear, perhaps, more strictly, like suspense. Or like waiting; just hanging about waiting for something to happen. It gives life a permanently provisional feeling.'[1]

Perhaps it was loneliness; perhaps I was waiting for Mike to return – or perhaps for someone else to come along to fill the void. Weekends could be particularly hard. During the day, James kept me occupied, and the household chores kept me from excessive introspection. Yet once James was in bed and the chores done, then Thursday, Friday and Saturday evenings felt long and lonely. Sometimes I would read, other times I would listen to cassettes or the radio, or watch television while working on a cross-stitch project. This was OK, but I missed the companionship of spending time with Mike – going out together, chatting, or just sitting at home playing Scrabble.

My restlessness increased when another woman who had helped with the McMaster VCF since Mike's death was appointed as staff worker. While I rejoiced to hear that the work was carrying on, it became apparent that I ought to phase out my involvement. Most of the people on the area committee who had supported Mike left the committee in the autumn, and I realised that it was time for me to move on as well. I no longer belonged.

However, my parents helped a lot. They often came to stay at weekends, or I went to visit them. They helped look after James so that I could go out. I was asked to speak on grief and bereavement at a workshop for the North American Association of Christians in Social Work at their annual convention; and reviewing my experience helped me identify some helpful things (and some not so helpful things) that a Christian counsellor could say or do for someone who had lost a loved one.

David and Robin were also a major help, as they often invited me over to their house at weekends. On the one hand, I could help Robin with childcare and with meals – she had just given birth to a baby sister for Ben – and on the other, we could be company for each other while David worked late. Also, James and Ben kept each other occupied. Therefore it worked out well, and we all had a good time. I even made the effort of cooking some meals for them – it seemed so much more worthwhile to bother to cook for others and not just for me. London, Ontario, where they lived was only a drive of about one and a half hours, so it was not an arduous journey to get to see them.

When James was about eighteen months old and beginning to talk, we returned from one particularly lively weekend with them; James had played non-stop with his cousin Ben and we'd all had a good time. I put James to bed as soon as we got home as he had already fallen asleep in the car. The following morning we were back to our usual routine: I picked James up and brought him into my bed for a morning cuddle before we got dressed and ready for the day. James looked at me and at the empty pillow beside me in my double bed, and said in his limited vocabulary, 'Mummy, you no have daddy?'

I looked at him in wonder. He was still just a baby, how could he have figured that out? 'How did you know that?' I asked. Then it dawned on me that he had toddled into Robin's and David's bed with Ben the previous morning. 'No,' I explained, 'you don't have a daddy; your daddy died; he's with God now.' I just didn't know what to say. James listened to me and nodded, then said, very matter-of-factly, 'Daddy gone God. Let's play teddy.'

My heart was in my mouth; tears welled up in my eyes, but James was ready to move on to playing teddy. Thus began our way of talking about Daddy, easily, whenever he came to mind. It seemed more sensible to talk naturally to James about his father as he grew older, rather than waiting until he was much older and it becoming a 'heavy talk'. I felt liberated to be able to talk to James about Mike, and to tell him how proud his father was of him. I knew that James would never know him as I did, but it was healthy for his own self-image for him to be able to be proud of his father and to have some idea of what he was like.

Yet the restlessness still continued, so I threw myself more and more into my work. In many ways, it was challenging and interesting. Providing psychotherapy to patients suffering from all types of depression and anxiety brought some reward as I watched many improve in health and in their personal and social situations. It was also interesting to talk to the many patients who had unresolved losses in their pasts. One woman was admitted with depression as a result of the recent break-up of her relationship with her boyfriend. When I took her history and asked about her parents, she would only speak of her mother. I questioned her about her father, and she would only say that he had gone. I asked her if she meant that he had died. She jumped at me in anger and said, 'Don't use that word! I just say that he went away.' I acknowledged that it was hard to talk about the loss of someone close.

Gradually, as we talked more about loss, she was able to identify some of her feelings of abandonment and anger, as well as a fear of trusting others in case they too might hurt her by suddenly dying.

Nevertheless, work was also frustrating. So often I could see spiritual issues involved in people's situations and I longed to share with them the hope and encouragement I had found in God and in fellowship with other Christians. A thorough psychiatric assessment included identification of a person's religious/church background. This occasionally opened up opportunities for me to talk about their beliefs, but I had to be very careful about what I said. I was their social worker, not their chaplain, and I was not to proselytise. I understood that it was important for me to be very sensitive to people, especially those who were vulnerable with illness and hurts, and not to take advantage of them or persuade them about something they weren't interested in; but I longed to have the freedom to be more bold and open about my faith. My inner sense of calling to encourage people in their faith wasn't being satisfied by psychiatric social work.

Needless to say, this awareness just increased my discontent – and it was now coming up to the second anniversary of Mike's death. Special occasions and anniversaries were still difficult – in some ways, they were even harder than the first year, when I had *expected* them to be difficult and had geared myself up for them. Planning something in particular on a special date or anniversary was a help – there was no use pretending that the day was just like any other when it wasn't. This year I couldn't go back to England; after the two visits of the previous year, I needed to save up again before I could make the next trip. Instead, I decided to visit Mike's grave in acknowledgment of the anniversary of his death, so I took James to Toronto to visit my parents for a few days.

Don Posterski, Mike's old boss, offered to come with me, and we bundled into our coats to drive to the cemetery. It was strange coming back to this place where two years ago we left Mike's remains. Unlike that day, when the snow swirled down, it was very mild for this visit. Just as we arrived, it started to drizzle. We didn't have umbrellas, so we pulled our collars up round our necks to keep as warm and dry as possible. We found Mike's headstone lying flat on the ground by the shrubs. It was the first time I had seen it engraved. It said simply: 'Michael J. Hare, 1960–1987'. Don said a prayer with me, and helped me put some roses around his grave. Then Don stepped back, and left me for a few moments on my own. By now, the rain was falling quite hard.

I looked down at the stone, so cold and lifeless. Mike was equally cold and dead, yet I still missed him so much. Tears poured down my face, mingling with the raindrops. Once again I said, 'Goodbye, Mike.' Then I whispered a prayer, 'Thank you, Lord, for Mike, thank you too for helping us carry on without him so far. But I still need your help to carry on. I have stayed in the same place for two years now, not just one. Is there any other future for me, an opportunity for Christian service of some sort, or the possibility of a new relationship? Or is this my lot? Please help me to be content if this is where you want me to stay, or show me the way forward if that is your will.' There seemed no reason to stay any longer, for we were both getting soaked to the skin. Silently, Don and I turned back to the car to drive home.

In the weeks that followed, the inner restlessness persisted, despite my work and my involvement at church and with friends; in fact, instead of subsiding, the restlessness seemed to increase in intensity, and I found myself wondering if I should be considering a new job or location. Yet I had a well-paid job that was interesting, and I had made a couple of friends on the psychiatric unit. James and I were settled in our little house. My lodger, Carol, had moved out in the summer to get married, but I was slowly getting used to being on my own. Neighbours were friendly and helpful, and I had many friends in the area connected with IVCF and church; I was also quite active in our local church. All in all, it seemed quite strange that I wanted to move on.

Yet no matter how hard I tried to put the ideas of change out of my head, they kept returning with an increasing insistence. I kept all these thoughts to myself, not knowing what I could do, and not having any idea of other possibilities. Therefore outwardly, our routine was maintained, and I continued to plod along until one day, out of the blue, my brother David made a startling suggestion.

He and Robin had just discovered that Robin was expecting their third child, and they felt the need to buy a larger house. He went on to say, 'Since you have been coming over to visit so often at weekends anyway, how would you like to move to London [in Ontario] and jointly buy a bigger house with us?'

I gaped at this incredible suggestion as he continued. 'You don't have to give us an answer right away, but think about it. It might be beneficial to us all – you and Robin could be company for each other, I could be a father figure for James, and the kids would have fun playing with each other.'

Was this what I was waiting for? It would certainly be a dramatic change. But could I give up the security of my present job and my network of friends and acquaintances, who had seen me through the last couple of years since Mike's death? Is this of you, God? I asked. The more I thought about the idea, the more it seemed like a wonderful opportunity. I knew without doubt that I was ready for a change.

9

New Beginnings

'. . . put [your] hope in God, who richly provides us
with everything for our enjoyment' (1 Timothy 6:17).

he very first house we viewed seemed perfect: only
vo years old, personally built by the owner himself,
eautifully internally decorated in off-white, and with
rey carpeting throughout. We opened the door to a clean
nd bright hallway. Up the winding staircase with light
ak railings, there were four good-sized bedrooms with
vo bathrooms, one attached to the master bedroom. The
aain floor boasted a large lounge-diner, a family room
'ith fireplace and a separate loo. But what absolutely sold
 to Robin and me was the bright and airy eat-in kitchen
'ith a walk-in pantry. Robin and I wandered into each
)om 'oohing' and 'ahhing' at each new wonder. David
owned at us and said in a loud whisper, 'Stop sounding
) amazed! You're supposed to be cool. You don't want
1em to think we're too impressed – they might put the
rice up!' But he admitted that he also liked it a lot.
  Over the next couple of days, we looked at other prop-
rties, but kept coming back to the first one. Impulsively,
'e made an offer and started proceedings to put our
!spective homes on the market.
  I told my friend at work, Gloria, about our plans.
We're going to move to London in Ontario, Gloria. I'll

be sharing a house with my brother David and his wife Robin.'

'Oh Catherine, I'll be sad when you go! But you deserve a chance to start a new life,' she said.

Two days after we made the offer, I received a telephone call from Robin – they had sold their house already! I was amazed. My estate agent had warned me that selling my house might take a little while because the housing market had recently slumped dramatically. Many home owners in Toronto were having to drop their prices, often needing to sell at a significantly lower price than that at which they had bought. In Hamilton, I was closer to Toronto than David and Robin, and so would be more affected by the urban market trends.

Nevertheless, I took their sale to be a sign that God was leading us in this direction. I waited expectantly for a buyer to appear for my house as well, but weeks sailed by and no one seemed interested. I became increasingly nervous – we had made a firm offer to buy in March. It was legally binding, and I needed the money from this house to put down on the new one. What would I do if I couldn't sell my house in time? I was wary of taking on an expensive bridging loan. Not for the first time, I moaned about having the full responsibility of the decision on my shoulders alone. How I wished Mike was here to share the insecurity, and encourage my trust in God and his leading. Yet, I admitted, if he had been here, I probably wouldn't have been moving anyway!

It was hard work keeping my house neat and clean with an active toddler eating and playing and messing it up. On work mornings, I rose early to prepare breakfast. We ate quickly and then I washed up, put the dishes away, and did a short tidy-up and whip-round with the vacuum cleaner – all before taking James to a neighbour on my way to work. Each night I returned home hoping to hear that someone had come look at the house, but no buyers were forthcoming.

After about eight weeks of this rushed routine, two couples expressed interest in my house and I put extra effort into my cleaning and tidying so it would be presented in its best light when the estate agent showed them over it at the weekend. I even re-folded all the towels and linen in the airing cupboard so that their corners perfectly lined up! But neither couple wanted to buy it; both considered the house too small for their families, and decided to look elsewhere. I had to sell my house within twelve weeks: now there were only four weeks left. I became very worried. Was there anything else I could or should be doing? I felt so helpless, so vulnerable to market forces. Another fortnight went by; the strain was beginning to tell. Gloria saw how worried I was, and every morning she asked how things were going. In my hurry in the mornings, I had stopped bothering to put on make-up and just threw on whatever clothes came to hand.

That night as I lay on my bed, waiting for sleep to blank out my anxious thoughts, I brought my concerns before God. 'Lord, I'm sorry. I haven't been trusting you. You have told me that I shouldn't be anxious about anything, but to bring my needs to you and you will take care of them [Philippians 4:6]. You know my concern, Lord. If it is your will that I am to move in with David and Robin, please help me find a buyer for this house. Thank you for watching over James and me this far.' A supernatural calmness and quietness came over me. With the knowledge that I had done my part, I could safely leave it in God's hands. Whether the house sold or not, it would work out somehow. With relief, I turned over and fell into a deep sleep.

The next morning I felt rested and relaxed, and once

more took some trouble with my appearance. Gloria mus
have seen an improvement in my clothes and a change
in my expression, because she took one look at me and
exclaimed, 'Catherine, you've sold your house!'

I laughed. 'No, actually I haven't. I've just decided to
stop worrying about it. As a Christian, I'm supposed to
be trusting God, and so I have left it in his hands. If it is to
happen, then he will look after it.' Gloria didn't share my
Christian faith, but was impressed with the change in my
demeanour and said thoughtfully, 'I believe something
will turn up.'

That weekend, a couple made an offer on my house.
Not only had my estate agent managed to make a sale,
but he had sold it for the equivalent of £20,000 more than
I had paid for it. 'You did it again, God, thank you! But
why do you always seem to work last minute? It's not
that I'm complaining – I'm greatly pleased – I guess you
want me to know when it is you who has accomplished
something.' God was again teaching me, step by step, to
depend on him. God was in control and would provide
for our needs.

It helped to know that God was watching over us, when
I realised that we were definitely going to go through
with our plans. There was no turning back now. So,
in faith, I handed in my notice after four and a half
years of working at the hospital, having received a
good salary and acquired much useful experience. It
was hard to say goodbye to the other social workers in
the hospital – they had been such a support to me after
my loss. I also said goodbye to neighbours and friends
and folk at the church, my home group and folk from the
McMaster VCF. It was frightening leaving the security
of their kindness and support, and their knowledge of
my situation and the shared remembrances of Mike. I
knew that I was embarking on a new phase in my
life. In London, Ontario, no one knew Mike; I would

no longer be known as his widow, never mind his wife – I would just be Catherine Hare, single woman and mother.

In a few short weeks, David and I rented a removal van and I packed up my furniture and belongings and off we trekked to our new home. It was all very exciting; I could hardly believe it was happening. It took a couple of days to sort ourselves out, but we soon found places for everything and felt comfortable in our new home. The children thought it was all great fun, and we enjoyed going for walks and playing games together. We decided to divide up the chores to help in the smooth running of the house. I took over the grocery shopping and the cooking – Robin wasn't especially fond of cooking, and I enjoyed having someone to cook for. Also, it made sense for one person to be in charge of it. Robin decided she would be responsible for cleaning the bathrooms and doing the washing. David was put in charge of the vacuuming, since Robin and I both had bad backs. We shared the childcare, taking turns in bathing the children and reading bedtime stories. It helped that David and Robin already knew the town, so they helped me find a doctor and dentist and to learn my way around the shops, discover the local family activities, and the various services in the community.

Now all I had to do was find a new job. Although there weren't a lot of job vacancies, I had good social-work qualifications and experience, so I hoped I wouldn't have too much difficulty in finding something. One drawback was that I was looking for a part-time position, which wasn't easy in the social-work field, unless one was willing to work nights and weekends, usually in a residential setting. Yet I believed that God had led David, Robin and I to move in together, so, expectantly, I started sending my CV to various social-work agencies. London, Ontario, was also a university town, and had three teaching hospitals. There seemed to be plenty of opportunities for medical social work.

Within a few weeks, I was called for an interview at the university hospital for a part-time position in their social-work department, serving those with multiple sclerosis. Since my uncle was afflicted with this disease, I knew a bit about it, and because I had several years of hospital experience, I was optimistic about being offered the job.

My first interview was with the head of the department, and he was very encouraging. Next I had an interview with the social worker who currently occupied the post. She seemed rather diffident. For several weeks I waited to hear from them, but – surprisingly – I received neither a telephone call nor a letter. Finally, I telephoned the department myself to find out their decision, and heard that they had given the job to someone else. Why did life always have to be so difficult? I thought. It was hard, but I was trying to trust God this time, believing that he would provide in some way or other. Then I remembered a saying that my previous minister, Dr Baxter, used to say. 'Pray as if everything depended on God; act as if everything depended on you.' So I asked God to lead me, and applied for other social-work jobs.

In the meantime, I was getting to know my way around the city and tried a few different churches. David and Robin went to the same church that they attended before the move, but I didn't feel at home there and thought I would try some others. Besides, although it was wonderful to live together, it seemed important that we had some separate social contacts and friendships as well. Attending a different church might provide such an opportunity to meet new people. Before I moved from Hamilton, the minister from my church there recommended a couple of churches in London that he knew of. One was led by a woman minister, the other by a man. Even though I was interested in the ministry myself, I was wary of attending a church led by a woman minister, fearful that she might be rather 'liberal' or too 'left-wing'. My own understanding of the role of women in the Church was still ambivalent: I thought a man should be the senior minister, and that women were more suited to team ministry or chaplaincy positions. I knew that this was ambiguous and inconsistent, yet my gut feeling was one of hesitancy. The reality was that in spite of my vocational leanings, I was culturally more used to a traditional church, so I went to the one led by the male minister.

I immediately felt welcomed by people as I entered. James was happy to go in the children's junior church, so I sat on my own in a church pew. The service was, on the whole, familiar to me and I felt comfortable, so I wondered if this church was where I should settle.

There were some notices on the back of the service sheet, and I read them with interest. One announced a vacancy for a pastoral assistant in a nearby partner-church: it turned out to be the other church that my minister had recommended – the one with the female minister! I was immediately interested. The notice said that the applicant should have some theological training, some experience in leadership development, and some skill in counselling. I couldn't believe my eyes – the position seemed tailor-made for me! *And* it was part time! If I was appointed, then God would not only be providing me with another job, but also an opportunity for Christian ministry as well – just what I longed for. Could this really be it?

In nervous anticipation, I telephoned the minister, the Reverend Karen Timbers. She agreed that I seemed to possess the required qualifications, and invited me for an interview, along with three other applicants.

First of all, Karen interviewed me on her own. She was tall and slim, and had short, curly strawberry-blonde hair, with a few faint freckles on her face. She was wearing a red tartan skirt and jumper; she was professional in manner, and gave the air of a mature and sensible person. From her description of the job and the questions that she asked me, I quickly realised that I was completely mistaken in assuming that because she was a woman minister that she must be 'liberal' or 'left-wing'. She was articulate and intelligent, and obviously had a strong deep faith, which she was seeking to live out in her Christian service. She seemed comfortable with herself and her role as minister, neither trying to impress, nor underestimate her role and abilities. In addition to a sincerity of faith, she showed compassion and sensitivity when I explained my family situation as a widowed single mother, and presently house-sharing with my brother and his family.

Karen showed me around the lovely old church with stained-glass windows and its beautiful stonework and wood-carvings. As soon as I looked around, I knew that I would love to work there.

I was then called in for a group interview. There were four other elders and other church members also considering potential appointees. I was impressed by the preparation work that the interviewees had obviously done before the interview. But I felt nervous and unprepared, and I was not happy with my responses. As I left the church, I felt totally deflated. Why was it only afterwards that I could think of so many more snappy and sparkling responses than the ones I gave?

When I arrived home, I told David and Robin of my disappointment. 'Oh well, it was a long shot,' I said, 'back to the drawing-board.' They duly commiserated with me and we chatted about the details of the interview.

Just then, the telephone rang. It was Karen.

'Catherine. I am happy to inform you that we have unanimously decided to appoint you to this position.' I was stunned. As I hung up, I shouted to Robin, 'I got the job! I can't believe it!' Once again, God had surprised me. It brought to mind Ephesians 3:20: '[God] is able to do immeasurably more than all we ask or imagine, according to his power that is at work within us.' 'Thank you, God,' I prayed. 'You are so good; yet I'm so slow to trust you.'

Robin very generously offered to babysit for James when I had to go to evening meetings. With my odd hours, changing from week to week with appointments, it would have been very difficult to find a babysitter. Now James wouldn't even have to leave home to be cared for. He could play with his cousin Ben; because they were so close in age, and thus at the same level of development, they loved playing together.

Working as 'Coordinator of Lay Ministries' (my official title) was indeed a rich and rewarding position. I was the first person to have this job, so I could mould it, to a certain extent, according to my gifts and abilities and particular interests. Soon I co-led a 'Spiritual Directions' group with Karen for some people who had come to her for pastoral counselling for various personal and relationship problems. My social-work training was most helpful in this group. I also assisted in leading worship on Sundays: sometimes reading the lesson; other weeks saying prayers or telling the children's story. Gradually I became more comfortable up front in the church. On a couple of occasions when Karen was away, she asked me to preach. It was so exciting and challenging trying out all sorts of new tasks.

An important part of my job was paying pastoral visits to those who had infrequent contact with the church, and also to those who were new in town. When Karen was away, she also asked me to do the hospital visits, and gradually I started visiting many who had been bereaved. One woman's husband only had a couple of months to live – he was gravely ill, needing an oxygen tank to stay alive. We talked about his impending death and how he had set his affairs in order. Another woman had recently lost her mother, and since they had been particularly close – spending some time with each other almost every day – she was finding her loss very hard indeed. A second widow had looked after her husband at home after he suffered a debilitating stroke, and felt deeply bereft when he finally died after sixty years of marriage. Yet another widow had been active with her husband in a church in a different community, but was relatively new in our area and felt terribly lonely. One elderly gentleman had lost his wife suddenly after a distressing illness, and felt equally bereft and alone without her constant presence and care. Listening to these stories was deeply meaningful to me, as I realised there were so many who were suffering from loss. Although most were much older than I was, it showed me that I was by no means the only widow in our own congregation – never mind in the whole world.

In addition, it helped me begin to identify some of the similar emotions and typical reactions to loss. I couldn't generalise my situation to others – each situation was unique. Unlike one of the widows, who found it particularly difficult to watch her husband suffering with a prolonged illness before he died, the hardest part for me was the suddenness of my loss and the fact that I never had a chance to say goodbye.

Nevertheless, there were some universal experiences and common feelings aroused through loss: sadness, loneliness, anger, depression, confusion and fear of the future were some of the most usual ones. I was learning much about loss and how people cope with it, at different paces and in different ways from each other. It was also rewarding to see my own experiences helping me to care for these hurting people.

After my first Sunday in the church, I never again

thought about the fact that our minister was a woman. It was simply no longer an issue, and I realised how culturally biased I had been. Karen was an excellent minister to work with; she was a gifted preacher, an efficient administrator, and a caring pastor – an exceptional combination of gifts. Also, as a woman, she became a role model to me, giving me encouragement to develop my own leadership skills in the church. I soon felt a sense of belonging in the congregation, and began to form several friendships. My vocational longings were finally coming to fruition and I found it a deep joy.

Meanwhile, James was fast developing into a little boy and was settling well into our new set-up at home. He had to share his toys and to learn to get along with other children of his own age, which was good for him. He tended to be a little passive at first, and needed to learn how to stand up for himself, but the give-and-take of family life was teaching him how to relate to other children.

In the autumn, David, Robin and I registered James and Ben for nursery school, held three mornings a week. It worked very well; I dropped them off at their school on the way to my fitness class and then picked them up on my way home. They loved the social stimulation – the singing, the crafts, the activities and the games. Now nearly three years old, they were both sociable children and eager to learn and do new things.

Before we knew it, a year had happily passed by. Ben's little sister, Elysa, went to the nursery school as well, and she too enjoyed the fun of the cheerful toddlers' class. Christine was born in the summer, so life in the house became even more lively with four little ones. It was a help to have some activities to keep the older ones occupied. I marvelled at how God had watched over us since Mike had died, and how he had met James's and my need of company in such a wonderful way.

One day I received a telephone call from friends from the McMaster VCF. They told me that they were about to have a mission with the Reverend Michael Green as key speaker. This had been a dream of Mike's – I still remember his delight when he showed me the letter he received from Michael Green, agreeing to come and do the mission. Since Mike died shortly after that letter, I thought it would never come to pass. But the VCF and other Christian groups on campus kept the idea alive and went ahead and planned the event. My friends informed me of the date and time, and invited me to come.

Robin looked after James for me, and I drove to Hamilton to join in one of the evening events. Michael Green was relevant and interesting and I rejoiced to see the enthusiasm and positive reaction of the audience. It was also a poignant time for me as I thought how pleased Mike would have been. I could picture him running around sorting out organisational details and getting up to introduce people. I met several students still at the university from the years when Mike and I had been involved – some of whom had even been in the accident. I rejoiced to see that they were moving forward with their lives, and that they had persevered with their education despite many months of missed classes and ongoing injuries limiting their mobility. A couple of others had now become leaders themselves in the McMaster VCF, and I was pleased to see how God had helped them to mature through their suffering.

After the meeting, I walked down past the theatre seats to speak to Michael Green. I personally wanted to thank him for coming after all these years. When I introduced myself, I was amazed by him instantly remembering Mike. He gave me a warm hug, and asked in a very sincere way how James and I were getting on. His recollection that I had a son made me realise that he was being totally sincere when he said he had been praying for us. I was deeply touched. Here was evidence that Mike's initiative and work was not in vain – that it still had an influence on others even four years on from his death.

This awareness of the usefulness of Mike's ministry was reinforced by a letter from the Ontario IVCF offices, sent to me later that year. The accountant gave me the incredible news that the McMaster VCF group in Hamilton had grown in leaps and bounds since the Michael Green mission. After growing from forty to eighty or so students when Mike was there, it jumped into the hundreds, as 500 to 600 students started attending a worship service in 'The John' – one of the campus pubs! I recalled the words of Andrew, our best man, at the thanksgiving/memorial service held for Mike in Britain. He had said, 'Your labour in the Lord is not in vain.' Even though Mike's ministry was short, it was still worthwhile. God hadn't removed the effects of the accident, but here was evidence that he was indeed 'working things together for good'. This tremendous growth gave me hope that some day, whether it be in this life or the next, God would fully restore life and make things whole.

During the next year with David and Robin, I felt settled in my job and comfortable at home. Life was very busy, and I had lots to do – the housework, shopping and cooking, looking after the children, and the various meetings and activities and visits with the church. I had little time to sit at home on my own and mope, yet every now and then I felt a pang of loneliness and would be deeply aware of how much I missed Mike. I had largely managed to let go of him, acknowledging the reality of his death, and the fact that we were no longer married, and had established a new identity for myself as a single parent, and a church worker. No longer was I generally sad and depressed. I had reinvested my emotions in new relationships: new friendships, and motherhood. Yet I still missed the intimacy and companionship that Mike and I had had together. There is something unique in the depth of commitment in the marital relationship, and more and more I found myself wondering if I would ever again meet someone who could be to me what Mike had been.

10

A New Love?

'We love because he first loved us' (1 John 4:19).

Will I ever be loved again?

As I prepare myself for bed,
Smooth on the rich moisture cream,
Brush my teeth,
Examine my face in the mirror,
A question begins to form:
Will I ever be loved again?
As I dress for church,
Splash on the perfume,
Select a pretty dress,
Try to look my best,
I wonder,
Will I ever be loved again?
I never minded growing old
Then.
He was aging, too.
We loved each other.
So what did it matter?
But now,
There's no man to love,
And as the years take their toll,
As my age begins to show,
That thought begins to grow.

> I was surprised to be loved the first time
> With my many imperfections.
> But now,
> The chances seem very slim
> That I'll ever be loved again.[1]

Suddenly, an old acquaintance wrote to me. It was Bruce, the handsome man I'd met through one of my flatmates in Ottawa – the man who had rung me up to ask me out on the same night that Mike first rang me for a date. Mike had beaten Bruce to it, so I had turned him down!

Bruce was now in Nova Scotia, about a thousand miles from Ontario, working as a student minister. He had attended the same theological college as me for a couple of years, and then went out east to do further studies at the college there. He had finished his three years of study and was now a student minister of two local churches.

He remembered Mike with admiration and respect, and had written a letter of condolence when he heard about Mike's death. I hadn't heard from him for a few years, so was surprised to get a letter a year after I had moved to London, Ontario.

As we wrote back and forth, we realised that we had many similar interests and activities in common. We both wanted to be in Christian ministry. We had both joined IVCF in our university days, and appreciated the teaching and fellowship we found there. Also, we had both lived in Ottawa and had some mutual friends and acquaintances.

Our letters became more frequent until one day in the winter he wrote saying he was coming to Ontario to see his parents in the town of Windsor, not very far from London, and wondered if he could visit me. It had been nearly eight years since we had seen each other, and so much had happened in between, but we remembered each other right away.

Bruce was just as handsome as I remembered. He was not quite as tall as Mike, but slim and fit. In contrast to Mike, who was fair with blue eyes, Bruce had dark hair and deep-brown eyes. He wore fine black-rimmed glasses.

We enjoyed a relaxed and happy weekend together, playing with the children, taking them for a walk, going to church together, and spending hours in the evenings chatting. As he left, he gently kissed me. I knew that we both felt a strong attraction for one another.

Our letters became more and more frequent and, in addition, Bruce started ringing me once a week. Two months later, Bruce came to Ontario for another weekend visit, and again we enjoyed our time together. On the Saturday afternoon, we took the boys, now aged three, ice-skating. It was fun having someone else to do things with. As we talked in the evening after the children were in bed, Bruce kissed me again. He put his arms around me and whispered in my ear.

'Catherine, you're attractive and intelligent. I like you a lot.'

'Thank you. I like you too.'

I was flattered to be considered attractive, and it was wonderful to be held again. But it also felt odd, after being married to someone else. A mixture of emotions swirled around inside me. I was very attracted to Bruce, and I was glad he was attracted to me. Yet kissing him reminded me of my time with Mike; I felt a pang of loss. It had been four years since his death, but he lived on in my memory. I found it poignant to come to an awareness that now I'd had another man's kisses to overshadow his. I still felt a loyalty to Mike, to the special relationship we shared, but the reality was that we were no longer married; he was dead, and he wasn't coming back. I needed to carry on with my life. I tried to focus on the present rather than the past.

It was difficult to do so over such a long distance, but Bruce and I started developing a relationship. We visited one another once a month, either by him flying out to Ontario, or me travelling east to Nova Scotia. In the next few months, I met his parents in Ontario and some of the people in his parish in Nova Scotia, who were both warm and welcoming, and Bruce met my parents. Between visits, our letters became more personal and romantic. We both enjoyed reading theology and often recommended books to each other. We compared pastoral duties and challenges in our positions. Bruce had two congregations for which he was responsible.

After we had been going out together for about eight months or so, we both realised that we cared for each other a lot, and knew that we needed to consider making a serious commitment to one another if we were going to continue our relationship. Could it really be that God was going to bless me with another husband, and a stepfather for James?

I went to England with James that summer, and thought about my plans for the future. We stayed with Mike's parents in Margate, and again we enjoyed the fresh air and visits to the seaside. As always when I visited England, English life beckoned, and I found myself feeling uncertain and confused, with conflicting loyalties. I talked to Mike's parents about Bruce. They were happy to hear that I had found someone new, and said that they in no way wanted to hinder our relationship, saying that most of all they wanted James and me to be happy.

I knew that it was a hard decision, one that I had to make on my own. I took a walk along Westgate beach by myself to think about my feelings and talk to God. 'Lord, you know how much I loved Mike. If he hadn't died, I certainly believe we would've still been together. If it is your will, it would be wonderful to have a new life partner. But I still love Mike's family and England, and it's so hard to let go. Please let me know what I should do.' There was no audible response from heaven, but as I listened to the swell of the waves rolling repetitively up on the sandy shore, I thought of the ebbs and flows of life, how the seasons continue their relentless cycle year in and year out. I knew that my life must go on. Perhaps it was time for me to let go of Mike in this final way. If I was going to contemplate another relationship, then I could no longer hang on to Mike as my husband. This meant that I would no longer be known even as his widow – I would be linked with someone else. This felt like yet another big change in my identity.

A book I read by another young widow gave me courage. In *After the Flowers Have Gone*,[2] Bea Decker considers remarriage. She says to want to remarry is a compliment to your previous husband. I could see how this was true. Mike and I had such a rich life together that I had an extremely positive view of marriage. Admittedly, it might have been because we had only been married for two and a half years, but we got on so well. We rarely, if ever, argued – Mike was so easy-going and understanding.

As I walked back to my parents-in-law's house, I spoke out loud: 'Can you hear me, Mike? If so, how do you feel about me getting married to someone else?' We had never talked about this possibility, so I had no idea what he thought. Within myself, though, I really did believe that he would want me to be happy, and would want James to be cared for as best as possible, so I believed that I had freedom to move forward – without him. Mike would always hold a special place in my heart, but it was time to allow myself to feel affection and love for someone else. Yet it was hard to let go not only of Mike, but of England as a place, and of Mike's family and the friends I had made over the past eight years since I had known Mike.

The day after we arrived back in Canada, I flew out to see Bruce for the first weekend of September, a long weekend. This time, James stayed with my parents and I went to visit Bruce on my own. Bruce met me at the airport. We were pleased to see each other.

That evening, before I went off to stay at his friends' house, we spent a relaxing evening in front of the fire in his home. 'Catherine, I know Mike was a great guy. It has been four years since he died. You've carried on so well since his death. You are an amazing woman and I admire you. We've grown close over these last few months, and share so many interests and a sense of God's calling in common. I want to marry you, to be a husband to you, and a father to James. I would like to protect you and help you and to be your partner.'

'I'd like to marry you too,' I replied softly. Further talk was stifled in our warm embrace. It was wonderful to be loved by a man again. I set aside my thoughts of Mike and concentrated on Bruce. It seemed such an ideal solution – a happy ending to my time of mourning.

On Saturday, we went out for a walk down by the harbour. We strolled past the small fishing boats and the pile of lobster traps unique with their dome-shaped wooden frames and woven ropes that ensnared a single lobster if it entered the trap in search of food. Eastern Canada had a certain charm, and I liked the community feeling of the small villages. Everyone seemed to know each other, and whenever someone was in dire need regardless of their own limited resources, neighbours would rally round to help. Perhaps because of the harshness of their lifestyle – the high unemployment, the poverty and their vulnerability to weather extremes – each town had developed into a close-knit community. The bleakness of the hills set against the blueness of the sea reminded me of the Highlands of Scotland where my father was born; I could see why it is called 'New

Scotland' – Nova Scotia. I wondered if I would be able to adjust to the lifestyle here.

As we climbed out on to some large boulders, we looked out over the restless sea. 'Bruce,' I began, 'I feel I ought to admit to you that I had some doubts and uncertainties about us when I was in England last week.' I told him about my love for England and how I had a sense of conflicting loyalties, that it was hard to contemplate a major break in contact with the people here, which would be the reality if we married.

Bruce was hurt by my doubts, and offered to pay half my airfare back to England so that I could try to sort out my feelings. Feeling at a loss for words, we each listened to the relentless crashing of the sea against the huge rocks. The unsettled nature of the sea mirrored my unease within. I found it hard to explain my attachment to England, and Bruce found it difficult to understand my feelings.

As my gaze rested on the swiftly moving waves, I was reminded of the turbulence at the bay in Ontario the morning that Mike died: the rushing and pushing, and my feelings of insecurity and helplessness. Why wasn't I contented now? No, more than that, why wasn't I filled with peace and joy? Here I was standing beside someone I was close to, and who had declared his love for me – yet considering marriage to him was a daunting prospect.

It wasn't that I was afraid of marriage. I loved being married to Mike, but it seemed so much more complicated the second time round. I thought back to when Mike and I met and fell in love; my life was so easy and carefree then. I held nothing back – with reckless abandon I would have gone anywhere in the world, and done any sort of job, just to be with Mike. But now I was older; I was more settled in my vocation, I had more responsibilities, and knew more what I wanted. Rather than feeling open and giving, I found myself being cautious and careful –

weighing up the pros and cons – and feeling somewhat self-protective.

We climbed back down to the road, both aware that there was a tension between us. I realised that it must be hard for Bruce to compete with, in a sense, a ghost from the past. All the love and admiration for Mike, and the support I had received from family and friends, only made it more difficult. I apologised for my uncertainty, and explained that I did believe that I had let go of Mike and thought I was ready to consider a new marriage.

'Are you sure?' Bruce asked. I nodded, and we kissed with every anticipation that we would be able to work things out. Together we walked back to Bruce's car, and drove back to his house in the town. Feeling happier, I returned to Ontario and spread the good news to family and friends. They all rejoiced with me; having wept with me through my sorrow, they were pleased to rejoice with me at this blessing of a new love.

In October, I took James with me to Nova Scotia to be present, along with Bruce's parents, for Bruce's ordination into church ministry. He had successfully completed his three years of training and his year internship, and was now officially being recognised for his calling into full-time ministry. It should have been a joyous time of considering our future and calling together, but something was wrong: we did not seem to be a couple. Instead of drawing closer together, we found ourselves drifting apart; instead of enjoying the short time we had with each other, we had quarrels and misunderstandings. I flew home feeling bewildered and confused.

I spoke to my minister, Karen, who acknowledged that there seemed to be some cause for concern. However, Bruce and I continued to write to each other as before. He telephoned me once a week as usual, and everything seemed to be fine again. The following month, I went on my own to Nova Scotia; I thought Bruce and I might have more time together to discuss our plans, and to enjoy each other's company. But again we had rows; I returned home to Ontario feeling both sad and discouraged.

Usually David and Robin went up to their room after we had put the children to bed, and I was left on my own to listen to music and read downstairs. This particular night, though, I found I couldn't concentrate on reading as my thoughts kept drifting to Bruce and our troubles. What was wrong with us?

I recalled our first meeting again after eight years. We had been instantly attracted to one another, and I admired his hard work and leadership skills as a minister. We had such interesting discussions together, and I knew that I cared for him. But why could we not get on when we were together?

One possibility was our different personalities. Initially we had laughed when we realised how very different we were from each other. We had each, at different times, done the 'Myers-Briggs Personality Inventory', and learned that we were exact opposites on all four scales. Whereas Bruce was an introvert, I was an extrovert. Where he observed facts and details, I perceived the world through intuition. When making decisions, he was most concerned about logic and fact, whereas I was more concerned about people's feelings. Finally, whereas I liked my life to be organised and settled, he preferred things to be open-ended. It is true that opposites are often attracted, and can complement one another, but we just seemed to conflict and misunderstand each other. Moreover, we didn't seem to possess the loyalty for each other that has the will and patience to sort out differences.

Why was life so difficult? Was I expecting too much? Bruce was very serious, but I longed for someone who was fun and easy-going, someone who could make me laugh – someone more like Mike. Mike and I had got on so well. Bruce and I had become tense and uncomfortable. When we tried to talk out our differences, we just argued more.

Perhaps our problems were exacerbated by the fact that for four years I had in effect been the head of my family and now found it hard to consider adapting to someone else. After being on my own, it was difficult to learn to accommodate to someone else's views and opinions. The added dimension of the parenting relationship with James was also a concern. We found we had different expectations and ways of parenting, and disagreed about methods and style of discipline. I found it hard to share this parenting responsibility, having raised James almost from birth on my own. I knew James and his ways, and we had already established our own routines.

Bruce and I continued to write romantic letters to each other over the winter months, and struggled to work out our differences, even going to see a pastor and counsellors for pre-marital counselling. In the end, we realised that we simply weren't compatible, and recognised that we weren't suited for marriage. With sadness, we broke off our engagement.

The congregation at my church had by now accepted my resignation, and I had already reduced my hours since Christmas in order to give myself preparation time before our wedding in March. I had already been given engagement and wedding presents by people in the church. I found it very humbling to have to get up in front of the congregation to announce that our engagement was off, after all their gifts and kind wishes, and to admit that I'd made a mistake in getting engaged to Bruce.

But it was only a fleeting embarrassment in comparison to the deep disappointment of my dashed hopes and dreams. For the first time since adjusting to the loss of Mike, I again asked, 'Where are you, God?' There seemed to be no answer, just unremitting silence. It had been four years since Mike had died, and throughout that time I had tried to remain faithful to God – and somehow I thought that God would therefore reward me for my faith and patience throughout, and restore my former happiness in a new marriage. After all, he restored the fortunes of Job and Joseph of the Old Testament after their times of trial. I had honestly thought that God was leading me to be with Bruce. It seemed such a perfect match – on the surface we had so much in common, and he had known and admired Mike. But I was wrong. I thought that I had grown closer to God throughout my painful time of mourning. I thought that I knew more of God's ways, but still 'his ways were not my ways', and I couldn't presume on his will.

Feelings of despair threatened to overwhelm me once more. After being supposedly 'purified by the fire', and having, I thought, grown and matured through hard times and increased in my sense of responsibility, it was a shock to realise that I was still weak and foolish.

Joni Eareckson (now Joni Eareckson-Tada following her marriage) encouraged me via her book entitled *Choices . . . Changes* by showing that one never gets to the place where one is beyond needing God's grace.[3] Just because I had successfully surmounted one big hurdle in my life, didn't mean I couldn't or wouldn't make mistakes later in life. I was still fallible and still learning. It brought me up short to realise that I was still more vulnerable on my own than I had admitted, even to myself. I still needed actively to depend on God, yet at the moment he seemed so far away. Although I couldn't feel his presence, I hung on to the knowledge that he was with me, and would continue to work in me 'to will and to act according to his good purpose' (Philippians 2:13).

11

A New Adventure

'Because of the Lord's great love we are not
consumed, for his compassions never fail. They
are new every morning; great is your faithfulness'
(Lamentations 3:22–3).

I had to decide what I was now going to do with my life.
Having already left my job, since I was planning to move
out to Nova Scotia with Bruce once we married, I now
needed to consider a different future. With Bruce, I had
been planning to go to theological college in Nova Scotia
to finish my third year and go into full-time ministry myself,
so I now considered this possibility here in Ontario.

Karen and I met for lunch one day to talk about my
future plans in the light of my broken engagement.
Karen led the way in to the restaurant, looking her
usual composed and confident self, in a smart blouse
and navy skirt. We sat down at a free table.

'Catherine, how are you? I've hardly talked to you
lately, we've both been so busy.'

'I'm OK. I've nearly cancelled all the wedding arrangements, and my friend Julie helped me send out cancel-
lations to all our guests.'

'I'm sorry you've had such a hard time, but I've got
some good news for you. I met with the elders this week,
and they want to offer you your job back.'

'Thank you, that's awfully kind of you under the circumstances,' I replied.

'It's not just me – it was a unanimous decision of all the elders,' Karen said. 'No one has made any negative comment to me about your broken engagement – I wondered if some might – but I'm proud of them. Catherine, you had to make the decision you felt was right.'

'You are so encouraging, Karen, and I'm really grateful for the offer, but I think I've come to a turning point – and I've already made plans to move out of the house I share with David and Robin.'

'Mmm . . . OK, I understand – but your job is still here if you want it.'

'Thanks, I appreciate that – I don't really know what to do, but I'm thinking about a couple of other possibilities,' I responded.

'Yes?' Karen raised her eyebrows in a question.

'Well, I wondered about going to theological college in Toronto instead of Nova Scotia, and training for full-time ministry there,' I answered.

Karen smiled and nodded. 'As I've said before, I think you'd be suited to parish work. You should write to the elders to let them know your intentions.'

'There's something else,' I began. 'It may be just a wild idea – I haven't told anyone else about it yet – but I've thought about it on and off over the last four years since Mike died – and that's whether I should move to England. I know it would be a big change, and I'd have to consider James – but he's nearly school age, and if I was ever going to move there, it should be now, before he starts school.'

'I don't think that would be impossible,' Karen responded. 'I know you like England – but you will obviously need some time to sort out what would be best. Meanwhile, we can pursue the next step here.'

Although I still had a big decision to make, I left

our meeting feeling lighter than I had done for weeks – perhaps there was a way forward after all. The following week, I duly wrote a letter to the elders outlining my desire to go into ministry, and was delighted to hear of their affirmation.

In the meantime, having completed the unpleasant tasks of cancelling all the wedding arrangements and notifying family and friends of our broken engagement, I longed to get away. I didn't want to be in Ontario on the day when we would have got married. Upon hearing of my broken engagement, Mike's parents invited me to spend some time with them in England. I reasoned that perhaps getting away would help me to think more clearly, so I went ahead and booked flights for James and myself.

As soon as we landed on English soil, my love for England was rekindled. The early spring weather was grey and chilly, but the love and care of Mike's family and friends helped me to put my circumstances in perspective. Mike's parents expressed understanding of my decision not to go ahead with the wedding and reassured me of their continuing love and support – whatever my future plans should be. They were interested to hear that I was thinking about settling in England, remembering that I had mentioned it a few times in the past. Without pressure and without trying to influence my decision, they helped me explore the possibility. They suggested that I look for some positions as a church lay worker in the weekly church newspaper they received.

One job opening sounded promising, so I sent a letter of application; I was further encouraged when the minister invited me for an interview. He was positive at my interview, but said he still had several others to see, and so would get back to me by the end of the summer.

It was healing to have time to rest and to think. Life was quieter with just James, and we often went for walks along the sandy beaches at Margate. One day I left James at a friend's house and strolled out on my own. 'God, where am I to go? What am I to do? I'm sorry that I haven't been keeping in step with you. Forgive me for presuming on your will, forgive me for being so stubborn and selfish. Thank you for preventing me from making a big mistake.' I tried and tried to pray, but God still seemed so far away. By the end of our visit, I felt no clearer about my future, but I had re-established my emotional equilibrium and was ready to pursue the two options that I was aware of. I trusted that God would lead me.

Once James and I were back in Canada, I applied to Knox College, Toronto, and was duly accepted into their Master of Divinity course. Nevertheless, I was still uncertain of my plans. Thoughts of going to England refused to go away. As much as I loved Canada and my family and friends, England beckoned as a new challenge, a fresh and different lifestyle.

To provide some relief from all these ponderous thoughts, I took James up to camp for a month in the summer. We enjoyed the swimming and the evening camp fires, and the fellowship with Christian friends. I met Cathie Nicoll, a fine woman who had recently been awarded the OBE from the Governor-General of Canada, and also an honorary university doctorate, for her many years of work with students and campers.

Cathie led the early-morning staff devotions. She read from her notebook, in which she had recorded God's working in her life over many years of faithful service. One morning she challenged me. 'Don't let your sorrows be wasted,' she urged. She recounted a time when these words were said to her, after she had endured a particularly difficult summer camp. She described how she was able to learn patience and forbearance from her difficulties, rather than to become bitter and defensive. Later, she was able to see good come from her efforts.

Her words encouraged me to learn from my mistakes, and to leave the 'sorting out' to God.

While at camp, I kept hoping that I would hear from God as to what he wanted me to do next, but no booming voice came down from heaven. It was as if ever since my broken engagement to Bruce, God had hidden himself from me; he seemed silent and unapproachable. I struggled with depression and discouragement. I found the waiting was so hard – I would much rather know what I needed to face, than be left hanging on in uncertainty.

In August, I took James to my grandparents' cottage in Georgian Bay, and continued to wait to hear from the church in England. Finally, the letter arrived, and the minister informed me that he had shortlisted me to two out of twenty, but had ultimately decided upon a couple, who would both be able to help in the church. Despite this disappointing news, England was still an inviting possibility. I was still uneasy about studying full time at Knox College when James would only be at school for half-days. It would mean that I would need to depend quite heavily on my parents if I followed this option. Much as I loved my parents and wanted to stay near my Canadian friends, I also felt that I needed to find my own way. Since Mike's death, I had stayed for two and a half years in the home he and I owned in Hamilton, and then house-shared for the next two and a half years with my brother and his family. It was now time for me to find a place of my own.

I decided to take the risk, to postpone my application to Knox College and to go to England to look for a job. I still had no assurance that this was what God wanted me to do; I was very much lacking in spiritual confidence in knowing his will after my mistake with Bruce. But I did know that even though God is concerned about the details of our lives, he gives us the freedom to make choices. Deep in my heart, I knew that if I didn't try to move to England now, I would later regret not having at least made an attempt. And if it didn't work out, I could always reapply to Knox College in Toronto in the winter term or the following year – by then, James would be at school full time.

So, in fear and trembling, and still not sure whether I was doing the right thing, I obtained the necessary immigration papers and passports and prepared to move. I wasn't sure if I would find a job, nor if it would work out, but off we flew anyway. It was hard to say goodbye to my parents at the airport. They had been so supportive to me, and I knew that they would particularly miss James.

'I'll be in touch soon to let you know how things go,' I promised.

Mike's parents kindly let me stay with them while I looked for a job. It was a warm September, an Indian summer. I enjoyed learning to find my way around the area of Margate. Douglas lent me his car, and I practised driving on the left-hand side of the road. One day as I was driving past a country field, I admired the bright red poppies on the roadside. I remembered the visit with Mike when I had noticed these poppies for the first time. It was as if they were bright smiles of encouragement, and they filled me with hope. Something would surely turn up.

One possibility arose within three weeks of my arrival, but in the end it did not seem suitable. My parents-in-law offered to let us continue to stay with them during the autumn in order for me to look for something else. In addition, Douglas arranged with their minister for me to help at their church on a voluntary basis. This gave me some constructive activity during the day, and some English work experience. I also enrolled James in a local nursery school. It helped a lot to have Mike's relatives and friends around as James and I got used to the English way of life.

Weeks went by and no other job openings were forthcoming. In the meantime, I visited parents who wanted to have their children baptised, assisted the church community worker with a youth group, and helped out at the mothers and toddlers groups in the church. These activities were interesting and rewarding, so at least I wasn't becoming bored or idle while I continued my job search. James too was enjoying his nursery school.

Yet I knew that we couldn't stay indefinitely. Mike's parents were very accommodating, but I kept worrying that we might be overstaying our welcome. I needed to find a proper job and a permanent place for myself and James.

By November, I was becoming anxious, and started having doubts about whether I should have come to England. Was it all just a pipedream? Was I subconsciously still trying to find Mike? Should I return to Canada at Christmas and go to theological college after all? To keep my options open, I contacted Knox College, who agreed to postpone my application till January if need be. After a lot of thinking and discussion with Mike's parents, I made the decision that if I didn't find a job by Christmas, then I would return to Canada. I would have been in England for four months by then; at least I would have tried.

Knowing my discouragement, Ann and Douglas suggested that we take James on a retreat during his half-term holiday, and booked us in for a week's holiday at Ashburnham Place, a Christian retreat centre in East Sussex, near Battle. A change of scenery was just what we needed, and we enjoyed the morning Bible devotions and the beautiful scenery of the enormous gardens and wood. We visited the local sights, and felt relaxed and refreshed in the peaceful surroundings.

On the Friday afternoon I went out for a walk on my own in the woods. The leaves had begun to turn, and had become a brilliant gold and russet. The dark-green heavy boughs of the cedar trees by the river stood out against this bright background. In appreciation, I thanked God for the beauty and variety of his creation. As I neared the small arched stone bridge over the river running through the property, I talked to God. 'Lord, you know I've come to my end. I don't know what to do. Should I go back to Canada or should I stay here? Have I been silly and impetuous coming over here? I don't mind either way – I'll do what you want, but I need to know what it is.' By this time, I had so little faith that I didn't expect any reply at all. I just hoped that expressing my feelings would have some kind of cathartic effect.

From the gentle breeze, though, came a whisper, 'Where you go I will go, and where you stay I will stay. Your people will be my people and your God my God.' It was a verse from the Bible – Ruth 1:16. At first I wondered why this verse had come to mind, especially as it seemed totally irrelevant and unrelated to my prayer. Then I remembered I had quoted those very words to Mike when we first considered coming over to England after getting married.

On that occasion, I had emphasised the initial sentence to him. My point was that I would go wherever Mike liked, as long as we could be together. But this time the emphasis seemed to be on the second phrase, 'your people will be my people'. I thought of the story of Ruth who originally said these words. She was also a young widow, lost and needing to find her way forward. She left her home and followed her mother-in-law back to her mother-in-law's people, the Israelites. It was as if I had spoken a prophecy to Mike, without even being aware of it. I wasn't thinking about becoming a part of Mike's family when I first uttered those words, but I could see how since marrying him – and even more so since his death – his family had become my family. We had become very close in our shared loss. Unlike Ruth, I did have a family of my own, in Canada, whom I loved very much, but this verse seemed to be God's assurance that he was happy for me to live in England.

It was such an incredible relief to hear God after eight long months of silence. As no one was looking, I raised my arms up and said, 'Thank you, Lord.' I rushed back to the lodge to tell Mike's parents the good news.

When I returned to the main lodge, Ann and Douglas were sitting in the lounge on their own in a corner. James had gone off to play with a friend. Since they were alone, I told them about my prayer and the verse that came to mind, but by now I wasn't so sure if they would agree with me that it was God's voice that I heard. Yet they listened carefully and nodded when I explained what I thought the verse meant. Then Douglas said, 'Did you know, that was our wedding verse – we went out to Africa as missionaries right after our wedding.'

That night I slept deeply and soundly, believing that God would open up a job possibility in England. The next morning James and I met Mike's parents at breakfast. A new man named Charles Earwicker was to lead the morning devotions that day. He read from Ruth, chapter 1! I gaped in surprise. He ended at verse 16. How could he have known? Ann, Douglas and I exchanged glances. I heard little of what he said after that – I was just so amazed that God would confirm his 'word' to me in this way. He knew of my uncertainty and insecurity, having recently made such a big mistake about his will for me, and he knew of my need for extra encouragement.

We drove home to my parents-in-law's house, light of heart, rested and expectant; I was once more able to be patient until a job turned up. The following week I was offered a job in the office of Hildenborough Evangelistic Trust, a Christian organisation providing retreats and conferences to those needing healing and renewal. Suddenly and swiftly my prayers had been answered, and the waiting seemed worthwhile.

James and I flew home to Canada to spend Christmas with my family and to say goodbye to family and friends before we embarked on our new adventure. A special treat was that my sister Fiona was also visiting, and we were able to see her too. At the end of our visit, James and I said a tearful goodbye to my parents and I promised to visit them the next summer.

We left for England on New Year's Day – appropriately, because it signalled for us both the start of a new year and a new lifestyle. James and I moved to a small town in Kent, the garden of England. Mike's mother had helped me find a fully furnished, pretty little cottage to rent, before I took James home to Canada, so we were ready to move in straight away. I started work the following week. I duly registered James in a local school, conveniently located just up the road. We soon met our neighbours and made some friends; and we found a warm and caring church to join, within walking distance of the cottage. In a few short months, I had learned to find my way around and felt settled.

Two years have now passed since our arrival in England, seven years since Mike's death, and James and I are happily settled here. James has grown up into a bright and sociable seven-year-old. He is in the top group in his class in reading and maths, and loves drawing. He has a delightful, placid nature – just like his father. Generally, I no longer find it too hard being a single parent, but mercifully I don't have to endure the real financial struggles that many single parents face. Also, church friends and neighbours have been a great help with babysitting.

As James gets older, I find that I enjoy him more and more. The plus side of him being an only child is that I can concentrate on his needs and spend more time with him. He seems such a happy, well-adjusted child; and I feel very relieved that I never had to deal with his grief as well as my own. I still find it painful that James never knew his father; but I have told him about Mike, the memorable and funny stories, and we talk about him naturally – whenever he comes to mind. It means a lot to me that James knows that he was held by Mike, and very much loved by him.

Although I have considered remarriage since my broken engagement to Bruce, I am still single. And even after seven years on my own, I sometimes find it hard. I still miss the friendship and intimacy that Mike and I once shared. Occasionally when I go to social functions on my own, I feel alone and uncomfortable when everyone else seems to be part of a couple. I still feel frustrated and helpless when the washing-machine breaks down, or the car packs up, or the gas or electricity supply needs attention and I am unable to fix the problem. There are times when it hurts to see friends going home to their husbands, knowing that no matter what kind of day they have had, there is someone at home who loves them and accepts them just as they are. And I still on occasions rail against God because life seems so unfair.

Yet on the plus side, I have many blessings for which to be thankful. In lots of ways my life is much easier than the lives of many people I meet. I have some very good friends – both male and female, young and old. I have also been blessed by a large and caring family, and James and I have lots of contact with both my family and Mike's. Our visits to my own parents and family are obviously less frequent because we live so far away, but we write, talk on the phone and try to see each other a couple of times a year.

After six months of working with the Hildenborough Trust, I started a new job as administrator at Monarch

Publications, a Christian publishing company. Sometimes I feel I am doing a juggling act – working and running a home on my own – but then I remember that lots of other women also have to do that. Generally, though, I enjoy the variety of my different activities. Also, I am very grateful to be able to work part time and to have employers who are so understanding and accommodating. If I am honest, I would probably have worked outside the home after James was born even if Mike was still alive. I seem to thrive on the social contact and intellectual stimulation of work, but I also love the comfort and relaxation of home and the fun of doing things with James. I cherish the time that James and I have together, and really enjoy spending time with him.

Recently I was invited to serve as an elder at our church, and I get great satisfaction from my involvement there: visiting people, co-leading a home group and a seekers' group for young adults.

God has indeed been faithful to 'keep that which I committed' to him long ago. When I broke off my engagement to Mark in my teens, I promised that I would follow Jesus regardless of my marital status; and God has given me the strength to do that. And whilst I would never of course have chosen to be widowed, I recognise that it has given me the opportunity to discover my own identity and my own leadership skills and abilities, and to find my own area of ministry, in a way that I probably would not have done if I was still married. Life has meaning, and I have found a sense of belonging in our neighbourhood community.

One afternoon after I had collected James from school, we walked past some brilliant red poppies in a neighbour's garden. Seeing their cheerful scarlet faces, I thought of the verse that John Stott had said to me many years ago: '"For I know the plans I have for you," declares the Lord, "plans to prosper you and not to harm you, plans to give you hope and a future"' (Jeremiah 29:11). God has indeed watched over us and given us hope. Life certainly hasn't turned out the way I expected, or would have chosen, but God has faithfully remained with me each step of the way.

If this was a work of fiction, it would have ended with wedding bells, but I am learning that life isn't always that neat and tidy, and fortunes are not always restored in this life. Tony Campolo, a Christian sociologist, 'refers in *Who Switched the Price Tags?*[1] to Hebrews 11, which gives a list of great heroes of the faith in times past. This list shows that a life of faith may be filled with joy and blessing, or it may be a life of hardship and sorrow. God recognises the faith of both sets of people, and will some day reward those who bear trials and persecutions with patience. God requires his followers to wait and trust, regardless of their circumstances.

So far in life, I have suffered loss and disappointment, but through these things I have had the privilege of first-hand experience of God's grace and his ongoing provision and caring presence. For many people, life is difficult and challenging, but I know that however hard it gets, life is still worth living because in Christ I have ultimate meaning and purpose. I have meaning because I am one of God's children and part of his church family. Although at times I may feel lonely, I know I am never truly alone. I have purpose because, having received so much love and mercy from God, I can't help sharing it with others who are lonely, bereaved and disappointed by life's events. This is something I find deeply rewarding.

With each new challenge I am gradually learning to trust more deeply in God's goodness and faithfulness to meet my deepest needs. I am still working out my vocational calling. My present work is stimulating, but I am also considering different possibilities for church ministry here in England. Perhaps I might pursue further training, or I might return to pastoral care and counselling. Perhaps in my ventures and travels I might meet someone new.

Who knows what lies around the corner? My future may hold further sorrows or unexpected joys. Either way, I can look ahead with hope and confidence, knowing that God goes before me, and travels with me, each step I take along life's path.

Notes

Chapter 4: Valley of Grief

1 Corrie ten Boom, *The Hiding Place*, London, Hodder and Stoughton, 1976.
2 C.S. Lewis, *The Lion, the Witch and the Wardrobe*, London, Collins, 1974.
3 C.S. Lewis, *The Problem of Pain*, London, Fontana, 1957.

Chapter 5: Rituals and Reflections

1 Harold Kushner, *When Bad Things Happen to Good People*, London, Pan Books, 1982.
2 Henri Nouwen, *The Wounded Healer: Ministry in Contemporary Society*, London, Darton, Longman and Todd, 1994.
3 Eddie Askew, *Disguises of Love: Meditation and Prayers*, Brentford, Leprosy Mission International, 1983.

Chapter 6: Early Days

1 Dorothy Hsu, *Mending*, Fort Washington, Pennsylvania, USA, Christian Literature Crusade, 1988.
2 Joni Eareckson and Steve Estes, *A Step Further:*

Growing Closer to God through Hurt and Friendship, London, Marshall Pickering, 1991.

Chapter 7: No Longer the Same

1 Dorothy Hsu, *Mending*, Fort Washington, Pennsylvania, USA, Christian Literature Crusade, 1988.

Chapter 8: Letting Go

1 C.S. Lewis, *A Grief Observed*, London, Faber & Faber, 1966.

Chapter 10: A New Love?

1 Dorothy Hsu, *Mending*, Fort Washington, Pennsylvania, USA, Christian Literature Crusade, 1988.
2 Bea Decker, *After the Flowers Have Gone*.
3 Joni Eareckson, *Choices . . . Changes: Moving Forward with God*, London, Marshall Pickering, 1991.

Chapter 11: A New Adventure

1 Tony Campolo, *Who Switched the Price Tags?*, Bletchley, Word Publishing, 1987.